KHUSHWANT SINGH (77), needs no intr
rian and journalist, he is much the most w
today. His three weekly columns are reproduced by over 50 journals in
India and abroad.

With 63 books to his credit, Khushwant Singh first shot into fame with
his award-winning bestseller *Train to Pakistan* (1955), which powerfully
depicted the mass hysteria and senseless communal violence that
followed the 1947 partition of the country. This novel was followed by
I Shall Not Hear the Nightingale (1959), a short-story collection *A Bride
for the Sahib* (1967), and the non-fiction collection *Good People, Bad
People* (1977)

Over the years he has lectured and written extensively on history,
culture, and philosophy. In 1966, he published a two-volume *History of
the Sikhs*, which now, fully updated, is still considered the most
authoritative writing on the subject. His two recent bestsellers include
Need for a New Religion in India & Other Essays and *Sex, Scotch &
Scholarship: Selected Writings.*

Also by Khushwant Singh
in UBSPD

Sex, Scotch & Scholarship
(Selected Writings)

Need for a New Religion in India
and Other Essays

My Bleeding Punjab

Khushwant Singh

UBSPD

UBS Publishers' Distributors Ltd.

New Delhi ● Bombay ● Bangalore ● Madras
Calcutta ● Patna ● Kanpur ● London

UBS Publishers' Distributors Ltd.
5 Ansari Road, New Delhi-110 002
Bombay Bangalore Madras
Calcutta Patna Kanpur London

First Published 1992

ISBN 81-85674-20-5

Cover Design : UBS Art Studio.

Lasertypeset and printed at Rajkamal Electric Press, B-35/9, G. T.
Karnal Road Industrial Area, Delhi-110 033

To
Giani Zail Singh
who stood for the Khalsa Panth
against fanaticism, and
for the integrity of India

Contents

Contents

Calendar of Events

August 1977 — Jarnail Singh Bhindranwale becomes head of the Damdami Taksal, launches *Amrit Prachar* campaign.

13 April, 1978 — Confrontation between Bhindranwale's followers and Nirankaris at Amritsar.

24 April, 1980 — Baba Gurbachan Singh, head of the Nirankaris, slain at Delhi.

20 March, 1981 — Flag of 'New Republic of Khalistan' hoisted at Anandpur Sahib.

9 Sept., 1981 — Lala Jagat Narain, head of *Hind Samachar* group of newspapers murdered.

20 Sept., 1981 — Bhindranwale arrested at Chowk Mehta. Wave of murders, bomb explosions, sabotage of railway tracks, hijacking of an IA plane follows.

15 Oct., 1981 — Bhindranwale released. More murders, explosions and shoot-outs.

13 April, 1982 — World Sikh Convention organised by Shiromani Akali Dal to stress that Sikhs are a separate nation.

1

Khushwant Singh

24 April, 1982 — *Nahar Roko* agitation organised. Desecration of gurdwaras and temples follows.

4 Aug., 1982 — Shiromani Akali Dal launches its intensified morcha: *Dharam Yuddho.* Two IA planes hijacked and Chief Minister Darbara Singh escapes bid on his life. Wave of murders continues.

4 April, 1983 — *Rasta Roko* agitation organised by the Akali Dal.

25 April, 1983 — DIG of Police, Jalandhar, A.S. Atwal shot dead at the Golden Temple.

June-July, 1983 — Number of banks and armouries looted.

6 Oct., 1983 — President's rule promulgated in Punjab. Bank and shop robberies continue into the next year.

14 Feb., 1984 — Hindu Suraksha Samiti organises a Punjab Bandh. It is marked by violence.

27 Feb., 1984 — Pages of Article 25 of the Constitution burnt by the Akali Dal.

13 Mar., 1984 — Attempt on the life of Darbara Singh.

28 Mar., 1984 — Harbans Singh Manchanda, President Delhi Gurdwara Prabandhak Committee shot dead.

Apr.-May, 1984 — Killings continue on a daily basis.

23 May, 1984 — Longowal launches Non-Cooperation Programme.

6 June, 1984 — Operation Bluestar to flush out terrorists from the Golden Temple. Bhindranwale killed.

31 Oct., 1984 — Mrs. Indira Gandhi assassinated by her Sikh body-guards. An Anti-Sikh Pogrom in Delhi.

31 Oct., 1984 — Elections announced.

31 Oct., 1984 — Congress-I wins a thumping majority

2

	and Rajiv Gandhi takes over as Prime Minister.
24 July, 1985	— Rajiv-Longowal Accord signed.
20 Aug., 1985	— Sant Harchand Singh Longowal murdered.
29 Sept., 1985	— Akalis win majority in the Punjab Assembly. Surjit Singh Barnala takes over as Chief Minister.
June, 1989	— Khalistani terrorists train their guns on hawkers of the *Hind Samachar* group of papers.
22 & 24 Nov., 1989	— Fresh elections held.
2 Dec., 1989	— Janata Dal comes to power. V.P. Singh takes over as Prime Minister.
7 Dec., 1989	— V.P. Singh visits the Golden Temple.
10 Nov., 1990	— Chandrashekhar forms Government.
6 Dec., 1990	— R.K. Talib, Station Director of AIR murdered.
21 May, 1991	— Rajiv Gandhi assassinated.
20 June, 1991	— Election countermanded 24 hours before polling.
21 June, 1991	— Congress-I comes to power. P.V. Narasimha Rao takes over as Prime Minister.
Feb., 1992	— Election held in Punjab. Less than 20 per cent voting. Beant Singh takes over as Congress Party Chief Minister.

Vatan kee fikr kar naadaan!
Museebat aaney vaalee hai,
Teri barbaadyon kay mashvarey hain assmaanon mein
Zaraa deykh is ko jo kuch ho raha hai, honain vaala hai,
Dharaa kya hai bhalaa ahad-i-kuhan kee daastaanon main?

—Allama Iqbal

Think of your homeland, you foolish man!
Of misfortunes that lie in store;
Your ruin is plotted in the skies.
Just look at what is going on
What we are heading for,
By recounting tales of bygone days,
What profit will you find?

Introduction

The political climate of the Punjab started hotting up in the latter years of the 1970s and came to the boil in the 1980s. By coincidence I was appointed editor of *The Hindustan Times* and a nominated Member of the Rajya Sabha in 1980. Quite a bit of what I wrote as editor and the speeches I made in Parliament dealt with the rapidly deteriorating situation in the State: the Akali-Nirankari clash, the rise of Jarnail Singh Bhindranwale, the *Dharma Yudh Morcha,* storming of the Golden Temple by the Indian army, the assassination of Mrs Indira Gandhi and the massacre of Sikhs in towns and cities of northern India. Then came the Rajiv-Longowal Accord, its betrayal by the Rajiv Gandhi-led Congress government, the prolonged periods of President's rule, the steep escalation and spread of terrorist activities to other parts of India. Even after I had left editing *The Hindustan Times* and retired from the Rajya Sabha, Punjab continued to be the theme of many of my articles and syndicated columns *With Malice Towards One and All, This Above all* and *Gossip: Sweet*

& Sour. In addition I wrote a number of articles for foreign newspapers and magazines. Rohini Chopra (nee Singh) who has compiled and edited many of my books has done a heroic job sorting out my articles and speeches, editing and putting them in the chronological order so that I could use some of them in this book. They truly reflect my personal views on Punjab politics and the mess made by narrow-minded Akali leaders on the one side and the deliberately mischievous politics of the central government led by Mrs Indira Gandhi and her son Rajiv Gandhi on the other. Between them they have brought all the progress in the most progressive state of India to a standstill, ruined its agricultural and industrial economy and reduced its administration and judiciary to shambles. It is a tragic story. Since I am an Indian, a Punjabi and a Sikh, my responses to the events narrated in this book are understandably emotional. For this I make no apologies.

NEW DELHI   KHUSHWANT SINGH

1
In Amritsar

"This is the most fertile land in the world; any seed you sow in it sprouts into gold," remarked Gurinder Singh, son of late Chief Minister of the Punjab, Pratap Singh Kairon, popularly regarded as the builder of modern Punjab. Kairon was shot and killed on 6th of February 1965 while travelling on the Grand Trunk Road some 35 kilometers north-west of Delhi. With him died dreams of a prosperous, united Hindu-Sikh Punjabi State. A year after his death, the State was split into three, Punjab a majority Sikh State and Haryana and Himachal Pradesh both preponderantly Hindu. With the seeds of prosperity sown during the Green Revolution which made Punjab the most affluent agricultural state in India were sown seeds of discord between Punjabi Hindus and Sikhs. One could see this as clearly as daylight the day I visited Amritsar a fortnight after the notorious Operation Bluestar carried out on the 5th and 6th of June 1984.

From the window of the aircraft descending on Amritsar's Raja Sansi airport, I could see a vast stretch of fresh, emerald green paddy fields flecked with snow-white egrets. A heavy shower had fallen an hour before and washed the countryside making it look fresher, cleaner and greener. It was a scene of peace and prosperity.

No sooner we landed at Raja Sansi, the illusion of peace was dispelled. There were soldiers in battle-green uniforms everywhere, stenguns slung on their shoulders, hands dangerously close to the triggers. Along the route from the airport to the Ritz Hotel I passed several groups of soldiers sprawled on the grassy kerb. At a major intersection of roads, besides constables on traffic duty, there were men of the Home Guards, Central Reserve Police Force, Border Security Force and the regular army. At one point there was a bunker made of sand-bags with the nozzle of a machine gun pointing towards the crowded bazaar.

They told me Amritsar was slowly but surely returning to normal. There were certainly crowds around cinemas and cafes where there had been none for over a year. The car park outside the Amritsar Club in Rambagh was full of cars, scooters, ice cream and *chaat* vendors. However, the bazaar inside the walled city still looked somewhat forlorn. I was driven from Gandhi Gate through Hall Bazaar, usually congested with people, without meeting any traffic and arrived at the main Clock Tower entrance of the Golden Temple in less than five minutes. Rolled-up barbed wire entanglements prevented my going any closer. It was from the back wall of the as yet unrepaired cycle-shed that I got an idea of what must have passed on the night of the 5th and 6th of June; its entire surface was pitted with bullet marks. And it was not even in the fighting zone.

It was 3 p.m.—an hour before the Temple gates were usually thrown open. There were hardly any worshippers. I washed my feet and went down the marble steps. At first sight I could not see any visible signs of damage. It was after a while I noticed that the marble flooring of the *parikrama* had been newly laid without any of the inscriptions in Gurmukhi and Urdu bearing the names of donors and that the verandah flanking it had been freshly patched and whitewashed. Then I noticed that the two towers called *Ramgarhia Bungas* built during the time of Maharajah Ranjit Singh, which had overlooked the Temple complex, had their tops blown off. A third, the water tower looked intact but had in fact been put out of commission. It was only after I had gone round half the *parikrama* and come to the shrine of Baba Deep Singh Shaheed, the man who had slain Massa Ragha, a desecrator of the temple, that I saw evidence of massive damage done to the Harimandir complex. It was from this side that army tanks had advanced. A part of the *parikrama* had sunk under their weight. The entire eastern side of the complex which housed the archives containing over a thousand handwritten copies of the *Granth Sahib* (many donated by Pakistani Muslims after they had migrated) and *hukumnamahs* bearing signatures of the gurus had gone up in flames. It was from here that tank cannons had fired at the Akal Takht bringing down its roof, setting it on fire and thus forcing Jarnail Singh Bhindranwale and his men to come out in the open and wage an obviously losing battle against heavy odds. It was the tanks' heavy guns which pierced gaping holes in the *Darshani Deori* (entrance to the viaduct to the Harimandir) tearing away much of the *Ilaichi Beri* tree alongside a shrine. The Akal Takht with all its relics was a total wreck.

9

Peoples' reactions were telling. There were a sizeable number of Hindus present. They seemed to be more interested in seeing how the Sikhs reacted to the damage to their Temple than seeing it for themselves. The Sikhs gaped at the Temple with unbelieving eyes. I could see no religious fervour in their faces; they looked as if they were going round a museum or a picture gallery. It was the same in the Harimandir. Hardly anyone paid attention to the *keertan*. After perfunctory obeisance to the *Granth Sahib,* they went round on the upper floors and counted bullet marks. Contrary to government contention that due to the army's self-imposed restraints, the Harimandir had escaped damage, I counted over two dozen fresh bullet marks myself including some that had pierced through metal covered windows and shattered glass-panes protecting fresco paintings. The Sikhs' faces were flushed with anger; some burst into invective against desecrators using earthy Punjabi abuse never heard in the sacred premises. A few put their foreheads against the bullet marks and broke down in sobs and tears. Back at the *Darshani Deori* I saw old women pressed to the trunk and remaining branches of the *Ilaichi Beri* as if it were a human being whose arms and legs had been amputated.

What once had been the Akal Takht had been fenced off by a wall of barbed wire. Mounds of debris lay heaped on one side. Two tall *Nishaan Sahibs* (flag poles) bearing the tri-colour saffron flags of the Khalsa Panth fluttered defiantly in the monsoon breeze. Little besides these flag poles was unscathed. People collected in small groups to hear what others, who pretended to know more, had to say about the army action. Wildly exaggerated stories of the heroism of Bhindranwale's men, of the number of innocent pilgrims, including women and children killed,

were heard with rapt attention. One young man drew
my attention to a signboard on a wall alongside the Akal
Takht. The army authorities had put it up sometime
after it had occupied the Temple complex and overlooked
removing it after it had been thrown open to the public.
It read: "No smoking or drinking allowed here." That is
what our jawans had been doing in the sacred premises.
Their nerves had become over-wrought; the stench of
the dead and the groans of the dying had become too
much to bear. Most of them did not even know that
smoking was anathema to Sikh sentiment or that the
courtyard separating the Akal Takht from the
Harimandir was a part of the Temple. Rum and cigarettes
helped to soothe their frayed nerves. "They walked about
the *parikrama* with their boots on," said one. "They shot
boys of 15 and 20 in cold blood after tying their hands
behind them with their turbans," said another. "They
gassed and burnt pilgrims hiding in the rooms along the
parikrama. You can still see the bones lying about and
smell the stench of death." Their minds were so inflamed
that they believed anything they were told. Even that
Bhindranwale had escaped alive and would soon come back.

The Golden Temple no longer meant the same thing
to the Sikhs that it had meant for the 300 years it had
been there. It still looked lovely with its gilded domes
and marble reflected in the waters of the pool
surrounding it. Monsoon clouds tumbled across the blue
skies and flocks of pigeons flew across as they always
had. But the spirit that had pervaded it seemed to have
gone for ever. The flower seller at the entrance said to
me: "There are no worshippers here anymore; they are
all *tamashbeens*—sightseers."

Meeting Hindus and Sikhs of Amritsar further
confirmed the irreparable damage done to the hearts of

two peoples who till recently had regarded themselves as one, given their sons and daughters in marriage to each other, worshipped in each other's shrines and shared each other's joys and sorrows. When I talked to the Hindus, they harped on the reign of terror let loose by Bhindranwale but did not mention the damage done by the army. When I talked to the Sikhs, they glibly dodged any reference to Bhindranwale's hateful utterances and the cold-blooded killing of innocents by his gunmen but dwelt at length on the wanton destruction of life and sacred property by the army. Their anger was more directed towards their Hindu neighbours. "They celebrated the destruction of the Akal Takht by distributing *laddoos*; they entertained the jawans with sweets, cigarettes and liquor. They did not give a damn about our hurt feelings," they said. A Sikh manufacturer of motor spare parts told me of his first visit to the Temple after the army action. "We were passing through Hall Bazaar when a Hindu shopkeeper tossed a packet of cigarettes over our heads to a friend on the other side of the Bazaar shouting, 'here's the latest brand of cigarettes—Bhindranwale mark'."

What brought about this terrible divide between the two communities which had appeared to the world as indivisible?

The story goes back to the birth of Sikhism and its formation as a separate religious community. Also to the history of the Harimandir Sahib, the holy shrine about which the Sikhs are understandably touchy and whose sanctity they are willing to defend with their lives.

2

The Harimandir Sahib

If there is one place of worship in the world which
welcomes people of all faiths and enshrines within it
a scripture containing hymns composed by Hindus
and Muslims of all castes and worships it as God
incarnate, it is the Harimandir of Amritsar. Jews deny
Gentiles access to their Wailing Wall, Zoroastrians forbid
non-Zoroastrians' entrance to their Agiaries, Catholics
forbid non-Catholics from approaching their sacred relics,
Hindus bar the gates of their temples to Muslims and
Christians (and till recently to people of low-castes as
well). Muslims deny non-Muslims admission to Mecca
and Medina. Only the doors of the Harimandir, popularly
known as the Darbar Sahib and the Golden Temple, are
open to everyone, no matter what race or religion he or
she belongs to. Everyone can participate in the worship
that goes on almost round the clock and everyone can
get a free meal at the *Guru ka Langar*—the guru's kitchen.

Just as Sikhism is itself an edifice built of Hindu bricks and Muslim mortar, so also the Sikhs' holiest shrine bears witness to its Hindu-Muslim genealogy. The third of the Sikh's ten gurus, Guru Amar Das, received the site of the land as a gift on his daughter's wedding from Emperor Akbar. Guru Amar Das's son-in-law, Ram Das, who had represented the guru in the Mughal court had a tank dug in the place. When he succeeded his father-in-law as the fourth guru of the Sikhs, he decided to build a new town around the tank. *The Amritsar Gazeteer of 1883-84* records that "in the year 1577 he (Guru Ram Das) obtained a grant of the site, together with 500 bighas of land, from the Emperor Akbar, on payment of Rs. 700 to the Zamindar of Tung, who owned the land." Guru Ram Das (1534-1581) shifted the headquarters of the Sikh faith from Goindwal to the new township which came to be known after him as *Guru Ka Chak, Chak Ram Das* or *Ram Das Pura*. He invited traders to set up their businesses in the town.

Guru Ram Das had three sons of whom he considered the youngest, Arjun Mal, to be the most suited to succeed him. When Ram Das died in 1581, Arjun became the fifth guru of the Sikhs. It was he who raised the Harimandir in the midst of the tank. In keeping with the eclectic spirit of Sikhism, he invited a Muslim divine, Hazrat Mian Meer of Lahore to lay the foundation stone of the Temple. Two aspects of the architecture of the Harimandir deserve notice. Instead of building the shrine on a high plinth as was the Hindu custom, Arjun had it built on a lower level than the surrounding land so that worshippers would have to go down the steps to enter it. When it was represented to Arjun that the Temple should be the highest building in the locality, he is reported to have replied: "No, what is humble shall be exalted. The more a tree is laden with fruit, the more its branches descend to the earth. By whatever way you approach the Temple, you must descend eight to ten steps, therefore let the Harimandir be the lowest edifice of all." The second feature was that whereas Hindu temples had only one entrance, the Harimandir had four—representing the four Hindu castes—Brahmin, Kshatriya, Vaishya and Shudra. All were welcome.

After the Temple was completed and the tank filled with water, it was given a new name *Amrit* (nectar) *Sar* (tank) or the pool of immortality. Guru Arjun composed a special hymn on the occasion: "*Santaan day kaaraj aap khaloya*: God himself came and did the work of saints; into the beautiful land and the beautiful tank he poured nectar ... bathing in the tank is equal to bathing in the 68 places of pilgrimage, to the bestowal of alms, and the performance of great purifications." A couplet which is on the lips of pilgrims who visit Amritsar runs:

Ram Das Sarovar naahtey
Utrey sab paap kamaatey

He who bathes in the tank of Ram Das
Is washed off of all sins committed by him.

The city itself came to be known as the "House of Praise", Amritsar: *siftee da ghar*. What Varanasi was to the Hindus and Mecca to the Muslims, Amritsar became to the Sikhs: their most important place of pilgrimage.

A few years after the building of the Harimandir, Guru Arjun retired to a neighbouring wood where under the bosky shade of *Peepal*, fig and *Neem* trees he set about compiling an anthology of sacred hymns. He welcomed contributions from different sects of Hindus and Muslims. The task was completed in the year 1604 A.D. and the

Adi Granth, as it came to be known, was formally installed in the Harimandir with a senior disciple, Baba Buddha, as the first reader or *Granthi.*

Mischief makers did not take long to fill the ears of Emperor Akbar with false reports that the *Adi Granth* contained passages vilifying Islam. On his way north from Agra, Akbar stopped near Amritsar and asked Guru Arjun to let him examine the Book. Bhai Buddha and another disciple, Bhai Gurdas, called on the Emperor and asked him to open the volume anywhere he liked. By a strange coincidence, the page opened by Akbar had Guru Arjun's own compilation in Persian:

> From earth to light God made the world:
> The sky, earth, trees and water are God's creation.
> Man, whatever your eye perceives is perishable.

The second hymn that Emperor Akbar examined was:

> You tied a stone to your neck,
> And saw not God who dwells in your heart.
> O infidel, you wandered astray in error:
> You churned water and shall die in agony.
> The stone which you callest God
> Shall take you with it and drown you.
> O Sinner, untrue to your salt,
> It is not a boat of stone which will ferry you over.
> On meeting the guru, Nanak recognised the Lord.

The eclectic character of the *Adi Granth* deserves notice. It is the only religious scripture in the world which accords divinity to compilations of peoples of different faiths. Amongst the oldest and the most revered contributors is Shaikh Ibrahim Farid. 134 of Farid's hymns are found in the *Adi Granth*. He exhorts people to turn to Allah:

Listen to the words of Shaikh Farid
O dear ones, come to Allah.
This body will be reduced to dust
When it makes the grave its home.
O Shaikh Farid, if you could but stay
The ceaseless swan flights of your mind
You would meet the Lord this very day.

If I knew that I would die
Never to return again
I would not follow the false ways of the world
Nor let my life be spent in vain.

In your speech be true, in your actions be right,
And spread no falsehood.
O Farid, tread the path the Guru shows.
What takes six months to quicken with life
Dies an instant death.
It is swift as the flight of swans in the spring
And the stampede of beasts in a forest fire.

It is a flash of lightning amid the rains,
And transitory as the winter hours
When maidens are in love's embrace,
All that is must cease: on this ponder.

Farid, the earth questioned the sky:
Where are the mighty captains gone?
"In their graves they rot," was the reply
And are rebuked for tasks not done.

541 hymns written by Kabir are included in the *Adi Granth*. As a weaver he used similes and metaphors of his trade:

hum ghar soot taneh nit taana kanth janet tumharey

Know you who wears the sacred thread
That its yarn is spun in my house?
You but recite the Vedas and the *Gaitri*,
While in my heart is His prayer said.

On my lips is the name of God
In my eyes shines His light
In my heart He has His abode.
What about you, O Brahmin,
When death comes what will be your plight?

We are as a herd of cattle
And you our shepherd from age to age
If you lead us not to pastures new
What sort of husbandman are you?

You are a Brahmin and a humble weaver I
Yet how did I this wisdom find?
You seek favours of the princes
On the Lord have I fixed my mind.

The Maharashtrian Sant Nam Dev (1270–1350)
has 60 of his hymns extolling his deity, *Beethal*, in the
Adi Granth:

Pure and splendrous He came
As a waft of fragrance
No one saw Him come
No one saw Him go.
How can one describe Him,
How claim to know the nature
Of Him who has no lineage?

The flight of birds in the sky,
The way of fish in the water,
Leave no trace for the eye.
The heat from the heavens creates a mirage—
These are all illusions
As is knowledge of the Lord of Namdev.

The spirit of Nanak, the founder of Sikhism, who
began his mission with the proclamation, "There is no
Hindu, there is no Musalman" pervades all the hymns
in the *Adi Granth*. Says Nanak:

Mehar masit sidak musalla

If you would be a Muslim true
Let your life these rules pursue.
Let your mosque be the abode of kindness
In it spread your prayer-mat of faith,
And as you read the *Koran* think of righteous acts.
Let modesty be your circumcision—your *troth* with
  God
And gentle acts the fasts you keep
Let the rewards of good deeds be your *kaaba*
And truth your preceptor.
Let the *Kalima* be your acts of mercy.
And as you tell the beads of the rosary
Dwell upon the Lord's commandments.
Says Nanak: The Lord will preserve your honour.

Musalman kahavan muskal

To be a Musalman is not easy
Only he who is one should make the claim.
He should first follow in the footsteps of the holy
And accept their bitter words as sweet.

Rid himself of worldly goods
As sandpaper rids iron of rust.
A Muslim's faith is to follow his leader
Caring neither for life nor death;
To believe that there is a God above
Whose will is Law,
And abandon all thoughts of self.
O Nanak, if the Creator is merciful
Will you become a true Musalman

Guru Arjun, who was the first to proclaim the existence of a third faith different from Hinduism and Islam nevertheless expressed reverence for both:

I do not keep the Hindu fast, nor the Muslim
    Ramazan;
I serve Him alone who is my refuge.
I serve the One Master, who is also Allah.
I have broken with the Hindu and the Muslim,
I will not worship with the Hindu, nor like the
    Muslim go to Mecca;
I shall serve Him and no other.
I will not pray to idols nor say the Muslim prayer.
I shall put my heart at the feet of the One Supreme
    Being,
For we are neither Hindus nor Musalmans.

All Guru Arjun's writings (he was the largest single contributor) echo the message of love and faith in one omnipotent God.

Bhuj bal bir brahma sukh sagar

O Lord of Mighty Arms,
Creator of all things,

O Ocean of peace!
Take me by my hand and raise me
Who am fallen in a pit

My ears hear not
My eyes have lost their light
I am crippled, afflicted
Like a leper I come stumbling to Your door
And cry for help

You are the Lord of the fallen
Above You there is no Lord
O Compassionate One,
You are my Companion, Friend, Father and Mother
Let Nanak bear the imprint of your feet in his heart.

The Harimandir was blown up by the Afghan conqueror Ahmed Shah Abdali many times and had to be rebuilt again. It was finally built in its present shape in marble and gold leaf by Maharajah Ranjit Singh (whose wife Mehtab Kaur built the shrine of the Sufi, Data Ganj Baksh in Lahore). An inscription above the entrance of the central shrine reads:

The great Guru in His wisdom looked upon
Maharajah Ranjit Singh as his chief servitor
and Sikh, and in his benevolence, bestowed
on him the privilege of serving the temple.
(Dated *Sambat*, 1887)

The Sikhs are understandably very touchy about the Harimandir. Any attempt to desecrate its sanctity

21

has been countenanced by the slaying of people who perpetrated it. For many years during British rule the Temple's affairs were looked after by a family of hereditary priests (*mahants*) who were more anxious to curry favour with the rulers than maintain traditions of the Sikh faith. They allowed the annexors of the Sikh Kingdom to enter the temple with their shoes on and honoured General R.E.H. Dyer after he killed upwards of 375 men and women at Jallianwala Bagh. This caused enormous resentment amongst the Sikh masses. The Akali movement of the 1920s succeeded in ousting the *mahants* from control of Sikh shrines. Since the passing of the Sikh Gurdwara Act in 1925 and the setting up of the Shiromani Gurdwara Prabandhak Committee (SGPC), the Akali Dal has been in firm control of all gurdwaras in the Punjab including the Harimandir.

Periodically, water is drained out of the pool of immortality and a massive 'operation–cleansing' (*kaar seva*) is undertaken to remove the silt accumulated over the years. Just about everyone, be he Sikh, Hindu or Muslim is welcome to partake in the service. When it was first undertaken in 1922, hundreds of thousands of volunteers who participated swore that with their own eyes they saw the white hawk of Guru Gobind Singh flash down from the blue heavens and alight on the golden pinnacle of the dome. Such was the religious fervour that the Temple aroused amongst its worshippers.

The birthdays of the Sikh gurus and anniversaries of the martyrdom of Guru Arjun and the ninth Guru, Tegh Bahadur, are celebrated with great enthusiasm in the Harimandir. The most elaborate of all celebrations, however, is of the Hindu festival of Diwali. (Sikhs celebrate all Hindu festivals). Sikh association with Islam was kept alive till 1947 by the selection of the principal party of hymn singers (*Raagis*) from a Muslim family. Till recently, almost a quarter of all pilgrims coming to the Harimandir, were Hindus. A majority of Hindus of Western Punjab did in fact treat the *Adi Granth* as their religious scripture because they could understand its language in preference to the *Vedas* or *Upanishads* which they could not.

What the Harimandir means to the devotees can best be witnessed near the main entrance of the Temple. Parties of pilgrims approach, merrily chatting and quarrelling amongst themselves. Suddenly, the golden dome of the Temple, rising above the sparkling blue waters of the surrounding pool, hoves into view. They fall silent as if spell-bound. Palms are joined in prayer; some are overcome with emotion and tears flow down their cheeks. They prostrate themselves on the ground and murmur their thanksgiving.

The best time to visit the Temple is the early hours of the morning (*amrit-vela*— the ambrosial hour) as *keertan* begins in the *sanctum sanctorum*—when the night washed by dew and stars gives way to the dawn. It is then that the message of Guru Arjun comes through:

Na koee bairee na begaana
Sagal sung hamree ban aiee

We have no enemies; for us there are no strangers. Towards one and all we have goodwill.

In the recent past, voices of hate, emanating from the vicinity of the Harimandir have driven most Hindu worshippers away from the Temple. Hindu mobs have smashed a portrait of the founder of the city, Guru Ram Das, installed at the railway station. In and around the Temple, Sikhs have spilt the blood of fellow Sikhs. People have begun to ask: "Was it for this that Gurus Ram Das and Arjun raised the Harimandir, the temple of God and Man?"

How have things come to such a pass? A brief history of the Sikhs would be illuminating.

3

The Sikh Psyche

The Jews are not the only people in the world who regard themselves as God's chosen race. India's 14 million Sikhs go two steps further and not only believe themselves the chosen of God but destined by divinity to rule, each one of them equal to 125,000 (*sawa lakh*) lesser mortals and a one-man army (*fauj*). Both the Jews and the Sikhs have known persecution; the Jews for nearly 2000 years at the hands of the Christians and Muslims, the Sikhs for about 300 years at the hands of the Muslim conquerors and rulers of northern India. It never got them down. A well-known Sikh historian boasted: "Where there is one Sikh there is one Sikh, where there are two Sikhs, there is an assembly of saints; where there are five Sikhs, there is God."

Not many Indians share the Sikh's self-esteem. On the contrary, they regard them as somewhat slow-witted rustics, good only to be used as canon-fodder. "The only culture the Sikhs know is agriculture," they say. There is some truth in these back-handed compliments. The Sikhs are largely farmers and soldiers and excel in both professions. They, more than any other people, have brought the Green Revolution to India by trebling the wheat yield of the acre and are much the most prosperous peasantry of India. Next to farming, their favourite profession is soldiering. During World War I, almost a quarter of the British Indian army were Sikhs. Even today, although under two per cent of the population of India, they constitute over eight per cent of the armed forces. They are also an outgoing and aggressive people with an innate sense of one-upmanship—anything an Indian can do, the Sikh can do better. Three of the first nine Indians who scaled Mount Everest were Sikhs. More than a third of all India's athletic teams comprise Sikhs. You can see them everywhere in India: driving trucks, buses and taxis, (which they do with the reckless abandon of Kamikaze pilots), shopkeepers, contractors, industrialists, doctors, lawyers, teachers. Because of their distinctive appearance (all wear turbans and beards), they appear to be many more than they are. But the last census estimated their numbers to be less than two per cent of the population.

The word Sikh is derived from the Sanskrit *Shishya* meaning disciple. The Sikhs are disciples of their ten *Gurus* or teachers beginning with Nanak (1469–1539) and ending with Gobind Singh (D 1708).

Nanak was born in a Hindu family. He was a precocious child and like many other prophets, spent his childhood taking out the family cattle for grazing. He was indifferent to his studies and instead sought the company of itinerant holy men, both Hindu and Muslim. He was the despair of his parents as he would not attend to the family business and squandered whatever money his father gave him in feeding the poor and the hungry. When he grew to be a young man, a marriage was arranged for him and for a time he devoted himself to his wife and the two sons she bore him. Then the search for the truth became overpowering and he abandoned his home to become a wanderer. He fasted, prayed and meditated. He pondered over the misery that the centuries of wars between the Muslims and Hindus had brought on the people of the Punjab. His study of the two religions also showed him that there was much in common between Islam and Hinduism.

Nanak travelled all over India and is believed to have gone on pilgrimage to Mecca. He spent his last years preaching and singing hymns and was acknowledged by both Hindus and Muslims to be a divinely inspired prophet.

Nanak's religion was an austere monotheism which disapproved of idol worship and the Hindu division of people into different castes. Above all, it was based on the work ethic: strive, earn and share your earnings with the less fortunate. He emphasised belief in the institution of the Guru as a guide, community hymn-singing and eating together.

When Nanak died in A.D. 1539, he had a following of people dissenting both from Hinduism and Islam. It was left to his nine successors to mould that following into a distinct community with its own religious beliefs and traditions.

Nanak was succeeded by a disciple but thereafter, all the gurus came from the same family. The fifth, Guru Arjun, collected the writings of his predecessors, added to them his own compositions and so compiled the Sikh's scripture called *The Granth* (the Book). Guru Arjun's growing following largely consisting of Hindu peasants and tradesmen attracted the adverse attention of the Mughal Emperor. The Guru was arraigned before the Governor of Lahore and sentenced to death. He was executed at Lahore in 1606. After the execution of their Guru, the Sikhs began to change from a pacifist to a militant sect. Arjun's son, Hargobind, who succeeded him as the 6th Guru, organised his followers into an army. The final transformation of the Sikhs into a fighting force came with the last of the ten gurus, Gobind Singh. In 1673, young Gobind's father, the 9th Guru Tegh Bahadur, was summoned by the Mughal Emperor to Delhi and ordered to accept conversion to Islam. The legend goes that he offered to show the Emperor a miracle whereby no sword would be able to sever his neck. He wrote some words on a slip of paper and tied it around his neck with a piece of string. When the executioner cut off his head, the message on the paper was read: *Sis diya pur sirr na diya*—"I gave my head but not my faith".

Gobind succeeded to the guruship at the tender age of nine. Later he described his mission in the following words: "to uphold right in every place and destroy sin and evil; that right may triumph, the good may live and tyranny be uprooted from the land." Gobind realised that to raise a fighting force from the peaceful followers of Nanak, he had not only to teach them the use of arms but also to convince them of the morality of the use of force. "When all other means have failed, it is righteous to draw the sword," he said. "Light your understanding as a lamp and sweep away the filth of timidity." With this mission in mind, he set about to 'teach the sparrow how to hunt the hawk and one man to have courage to fight a legion.'

On 13th April A.D. 1699 (New Year's day by the Hindu calendar), the young Guru assembled his Sikhs at Anandpur, a small town in the foothills of the Himalayas and baptised five of them known as *Punj Piyaras* or the Five Beloved as members of a fighting fraternity which he named the *Khalsa* or the pure. He made the five, who came from different Hindu castes, drink *amrit* (nectar) out of the same bowl and gave them new names with the suffix, "*Singh*" (lion). He made them take an oath to observe the five Ks, namely, to wear the hair and beard unshorn (*kesh*); to carry a comb (*kangha*) in the hair to keep it tidy; to wear a pair of shorts (*kuchcha*), worn at the time by soldiers; to wear a steel bangle (*kara*) on the right wrist as a symbol of poverty; and always to carry a sabre (*kirpan*) on their person. The khalsa were also enjoined not to eat kosher meat slaughtered in the Jewish-Muslim fashion when an animal is bled to death, but only the meat of an animal killed outright with one blow, not to smoke or chew tobacco or consume alcoholic beverages and to refrain from carnal knowledge of Muslim women. This was to ensure that while fighting the Mughal armies, Sikhs would respect the person of their enemy's womenfolk. After baptising the five, Gobind was in his turn baptised by them. At the end of the ceremony they hailed each other with the new greeting, '*Wahe Guru ji ka Khalsa— Wahe Guru ji ki Fateh*' (The Khalsa are the chosen of God—Victory be to God).

Guru Gobind Singh gave final form to the Sikh faith. He declared the institution of guruship at an end and enjoined the Sikhs to look upon *The Granth* as their guide and the symbolic representation of all their ten gurus. Thus the creed of the Sikhs remained the pacifist one of Nanak and the gurus whose writings appear in the holy book, whereas the practice of the Khalsa became the martial traditions of Guru Gobind, with their justification in the stirring message of the many lines composed by Gobind. Those who did not accept the changes brought about by Guru Gobind Singh began thereafter to be described as *Sahaj Dhari*—those who take time to accept the new faith or those who 'take it easy'. However, whether Khalsa or *Sahaj Dhari*, the vast majority of Sikhs were converts from Hinduism and relations between the communities remained very close. All said and done, the Sikh scripture drew its inspiration from the *Vedas* and the *Upanishads* and was construed as a simplified form of Vedanta in the language spoken by the people. Millions of Hindus preferred to recite *The Granth*, which they could understand rather than their own sacred texts which being in Sanskrit, they did not comprehend. The dividing line between a Hindu and a Sikh remained blurred. Sikhs visited Hindu places of pilgrimage, observed Hindu fasts and festivals, denounced cow-slaughter and continued to inter-marry with Hindus of their own sub-castes. Virtually the only difference was the observance of external forms and symbols of the Khalsa. However, that one difference was of vital importance to the existence of the Khalsa Panth and the only one which gave its members a sense of separate identity and a sense of continuity of a proud tradition of facing up to odds and overcoming them no matter what it cost—a do or die tradition.

Guru Gobind Singh's military career was not marked with any spectacular victories. Apart from winning a few minor skirmishes in which he defeated the hill chieftains, it was a long series of desperate battles fought against heavy odds. He lost all his four sons; the elder two were killed fighting, the two younger ones were executed. But neither defeat nor adversity shook the Guru's resolve to carry through his crusade to destroy the oppression of the Mughals. His faith in his ultimate victory remained unshaken. Once Emperor Aurangzeb, believing that having lost his sons and having been driven out of the Punjab, the Guru would be willing to make terms, summoned him to Delhi. The Guru answered the summons by a long composition in Persian called the *Zafarnama*—the epistle of victory. He listed many of the misdeeds of the Mughals and added a note of defiance. 'What use is it to put out a few sparks and raise a mighty flame instead ?'

Guru Gobind's last days were spent in central India with the Emperor Bahadur Shah, who had succeeded Aurangzeb on the throne of Delhi and was more friendly to him. While halting at a small town called Nander (in the state of Maharashtra) the Guru was murdered by one of his own Muslim retainers.

Guru Gobind Singh did not leave his followers a kingdom but he laid the foundations of the Sikh military might by setting up a tradition of reckless valour which became a distinguished feature of the Sikh soldiery. They came to believe in the triumph of their cause as an article of faith and like their Guru asked for no nobler end than death on the battlefield.

> With clasped hands this boon I crave
> When time comes to end my life
> Let me fall in mighty strife.

The Sikhs' rise as a military power was spectacular. Under the leadership of Guru Gobind's disciple, Banda Bahadur, they laid waste much of eastern Punjab right within canon shot of the Mughal capital. Banda was captured and, along with his infant son and 600 followers, executed in Delhi. But soon after his execution, bands of

Sikh horsemen roamed across the plains of northern India extending from the Indus to the Ganges creating terror and havoc. They measured swords with the Persian invader, Nadir Shah and the Afghan, Ahmed Shah Abdali. The invaders blew up Sikh temples and butchered Sikhs by the hundreds wherever they found them. But it was like cleaving water with a sword. The Sikhs retaliated by desecrating Muslim mosques, by slaughtering pigs in them and looting their treasuries. Ultimately they triumphed and under Ranjit Singh (1799-1839) became rulers of the Punjab.

Maharajah Ranjit Singh (1780-1839) is the biggest figure in Sikh history. He modernised his army with the help of French officers of Napolean Bonaparte's army, extended the frontiers of the Punjab beyond Kashmir into Tibet and inflicted several defeats on the erstwhile conquerors of India, the Afghans and the Pathans. He entered into a treaty of friendship with the British which helped him to keep their rapacious designs at bay. He rebuilt the Temple at Amritsar with marble and covered its domes with gold leaf. Since then it is popularly known as the Golden Temple and is the holiest of Sikhs' holy shrines.

Maharaja Ranjit Singh symbolised in his person some of the confusion resulting from the difficulty of drawing the dividing line between the Sikh and the Hindu. He was punctilious about observing the Khalsa form and even required his European and Hindu courtiers to wear their hair and beards unshorn, refrain from eating beef and smoking tobacco. Although he had *The Granth* read to him every day, he often worshipped in Hindu temples and revered Brahmin priests. When he realised he was dying, he wished that the *Koh-i-noor* diamond be gifted away—not to the Harimandir in

Amritsar but to the temple of Jagannath at Puri. When he died, seven of his wives and concubines committed *Sati* on his funeral pyre—a practice forbidden by the Sikh gurus but sanctioned by Hindu tradition.

The death of Ranjit Singh was virtually the death of the Sikh kingdom. His several sons from different wives were on notoriously bad terms with one another. The Khalsa army became a law unto itself. Provoked by the British, they fought two wars against them and on their defeat, the Sikh kingdom was annexed by the British in 1849 A.D. The last Sikh ruler, Ranjit Singh's youngest son Dalip Singh, a boy of eleven, was exiled to England.

With the downfall of the Sikh kingdom in 1849, the fortunes of the Khalsa went into rapid decline. Thousands of those who had joined their ranks for only the material benefits that accrued, began to give them up and were readily re-absorbed into the Hindu fold. It was generally felt that the Khalsa would soon cease to exist. The Panth was given a second lease of life by the British who decided to capitalise on the reckless valour of the Sikh troops by enrolling them *en masse* into the forces of the East India Company.

Lord Dalhousie, who formally annexed the Sikh kingdom observed in a note, "Their great *gooroo* Govind sought to abolish caste and in a great degree, succeeded. They are, however, gradually relapsing into Hindooism, and even when they continue as Sikhs, they are yearly Hindoofied more and more; so much so, that Sir George Clerk (Governor of Bombay 1847-48) has said that in 50 years the sect of Sikhs would have disappeared." It was Dalhousie who laid down that the privileges meant for Sikhs should only go to the *Kesadhari* Khalsa.

Sikhs did not join the uprising of 1857. Nor did the

Dogras, Pathans or Punjabi Musalmans. None of them regarded it as a war of independence as some Indian historians have tried to make it appear and singled out the Sikhs as the only community which did not join in. Sikhs had good reason not to make common cause with the so-called Hindustanees (U.P., Bihari and Bengali soldiers of the Company), because it was these mercenaries that the British had used to destroy the Sikh kingdom only eight years earlier. On 7th December, 1846, the Mughal Emperor, Bahadur Shah Zafar, proclaimed: "We got the news that the Sikh army in the Punjab had been defeated by the British army. Hearing the news I ordered that a 21-gun salute be fired outside the Royal Red Fort to celebrate the victory of the East India Company."

The English rewarded the Sikhs for supporting them in 1857 by granting them large estates in the new colonies and making special provisions for their recruitment in the army and the police. The economic advantages of being *Kesadhari* Sikhs checked the disintegration of the Sikh community and its lapse into Hinduism. On the contrary, the last decade of the nineteenth century and the first decade of the twentieth, saw a phenomenal rise in the numbers of *Kesadhari* Sikhs. This was however, providing the Khalsa a hot-house existence. It yet remained to be seen whether there was anything inherent in Khalsa tradition that would ensure continuation of the Panth.

Kesadhari Sikhs continued to enjoy special privileges in recruitment to services and separate representation in legislatures throughout British rule. It has been contended that the British assiduously tried to keep the Hindus and Sikhs apart. It would be more accurate to say that they did nothing to bring them closer together and leaders of both communities allowed separatism to grow. In 1877, Swami Dayanand Saraswati visited Punjab at the invitation of Sikh organizations and set up Arya Samajs in many cities. He was very critical of the Sikh gurus and described Guru Nanak as an illiterate *dambhi* (impostor). This inevitably caused widespread resentment among Sikhs. To countenance Arya Samaj attempts to bring Sikhs back into the Hindu fold, several *Singh Sabhas* were set up. In retaliation to the Arya Samaj claim that Sikhs were Hindus, Kahan Singh of Nabha wrote a booklet entitled *Hum Hindu Nahin Hain*— we are not Hindus. This booklet was widely distributed amongst the Sikhs. Between them, the Arya Samajs and the Singh Sabhas widened the gulf between the two communities.

Sikhs remained the English rulers' favourite sons till World War I and were employed as soldiers and policemen in distant parts of the British Empire. The break came at the end of the War. Retired Sikh soldiers who had settled in British Columbia (and spilled over to Seattle and California) were subjected to indignities by their white neighbours and the governments of Canada and the United States. The British government did not come to their help. Many returned to India very embittered and formed militant leftist groups. On the 13th of April 1919, a large gathering at Jallianwala, close to the Golden Temple, consisting largely of Sikhs was dispersed by gun fire ordered by General Dyer. It left over 375 dead and thousands injured. The Sikhs finally turned their backs on the British and were drawn into the freedom movement led by Mahatma Gandhi.

The immediate cause of the Sikh-British confrontation was over the control of Sikh shrines including the Golden Temple which had become the hereditary fiefs of priestly families who were often more Hindu than Sikh.

Under a newly formed party called the *Akali Dal* (army of God) the Sikhs launched a massive passive resistance movement to take possession of their gurdwaras. Batches of passive resistors of over 500 each led by *Jathedars* marched out to break through police cordons. They were savagely belaboured by the police, arrested and gaoled. At one time, almost 50,000 Akalis were in prison. Ultimately, the government yielded and enacted the Sikh Gurdwara Act of 1925 taking the management of all Sikh historic shrines out of the hands of the priests and passing it to an elected body of the Sikhs known as the Shiromani Gurdwara Prabhandhak Committee (SGPC). The Akali Dal remains to this day the Sikh's main political party and the SGPC their mini-Parliament. The President of the SGPC and the Akali Dal enjoy enormous prestige. Currently, Jathedar Gurcharan Singh Tohra, is President of the SGPC which now controls not only the Sikh gurdwaras but also innumerable Khalsa schools, colleges and clinics run by it. It has an annual budget of Rs. 12 crores.

The Sikhs maintain with pride that despite their close links with the British, once they threw in their lot with the freedom movement, in proportion to their numbers, many more Sikh passive resistors were gaoled and many more Sikh terrorists shot or hanged by the British than members of any other Indian community. By the time the Second World War broke out, the British had good reason to suspect the loyalties of the Sikhs. They were not far wrong. The bulk of the 'Indian National Army' including its first commander, which went over to the Japanese under Subhash Chandra Bose, comprised Sikhs.

In the years following World War II, the Sikhs were caught between the contending claims of Indians for independence and the Indian Muslims demand for a separate state of their own—Pakistan. The Sikhs stoutly opposed Pakistan. When riots broke out in 1946 and 1947, they suffered heavily at the hands of Muslims who outnumbered them ten to one in the Punjab. The partition line drawn by the British divided the Sikh community into two leaving half of them and their richest lands in Pakistan. Almost to a man, the Sikhs marched out of Pakistan to India and in turn drove out poor Muslim peasants living in East Punjab across the border into Pakistan. It is estimated that in the summer of 1947 over 10 million crossed the Indo-Pak border in a two-way traffic and almost a million were slain in the worst religious strife in the history of the sub-continent. From being the richest land owners of India, the Sikhs were reduced to abject poverty. From 1947 began a Sikh diaspora. They spread out to different parts of India and soon acquired a near monopoly of the road transport business as truck, bus and cab drivers and dealers in auto-spare parts. Many joined relatives living abroad in Hong Kong, Singapore, Australia, East Africa, England, Canada and the United States (mainly in the Sacramento and San Joaquin valleys). Almost 30 per cent of the community came to live outside their home state, the Punjab, the largest concentration being in Delhi. There are over 300,000 living in Great Britain, and over 50,000 each in Canada and the United States. A popular story has it that when the American astronauts landed on the moon, they encountered a Sikh family taking an evening stroll. "When did you get here?" asked Armstrong. "We came here in 1947 with the partition of India", replied the Sikh moon-dweller.

It will be evident that the seeds of Sikh separatism were sown by the Sikhs' own gurus when they gave them their own temples, their own scripture, their distinct appearance, the common casteless name, Singh. As long as Hindus and Sikhs felt threatened by the Muslims, they remained close to each other. The advent of the British removed the danger of Muslim domination and the two communities began to drift apart. The British nurtured the feeling of separatism by recognising the Sikhs as a people apart, providing them with separate representation in the legislatures and specific privileges in the services. All these were taken away by the rulers of independent India in the name of democracy. At the same time, the younger generation of Sikhs began to question the traditions of the Khalsa and a growing number began to cut off their long hair and shave their beards. It was feared that in a few decades to come, the Sikhs would lapse back into the Hindu fold and become Hindus believing in Sikhism. There is in fact very little beside the external hirsute form of the Khalsa Sikh which distinguishes a Sikh from a Hindu. That and his aggressiveness. It is said that a distinguished English scholar while talking about modern India had referred to Hindus, Muslims and Sikhs. A member of the audience asked him, "We've heard about the Hindus and the Muslims, but who are these Sikhs you have been talking about?" After pondering over the question, the learned scholar replied, "It is awfully hard to define the Sikhs. They are a kind of vicious Hindus."

Present day Sikhs' grievances can be traced back to the Partition and holocaust of 1947. The Sikhs were the worst sufferers of the division of the country. But for the first time they also found themselves in a majority in several districts of eastern Punjab. Aggrieved elements amongst them began to ask: "The Hindus got Hindustan, the Muslims got Pakistan, what did we Sikhs get out of all this?" Much as the Indian Government tried to appease the Sikhs, it was never enough. The Bhakra Dam with its irrigation canals, the electrification of villages and the agriculture university in Ludhiana where Norman Bourlaug developed new strains of Mexican wheat produced the Green Revolution. The wheat yield per acre was trebled and the Sikh farmer once again became prosperous. But the clamour against discrimination and injustice continued to grow.

Another phenomenon arose simultaneously. Immediately after Independence, an ever-increasing number of young Sikhs began to give up growing their hair and beards. This was more noticeable among Sikhs living abroad. However, when they were in larger, compact units as in Singapore, Burma and East Africa, the incidence of apostasy was lower than in countries like Canada, the United States and England where it was rare to meet a second generation Sikh migrant who was a Khalsa. In the preface of my first short history, *The Sikhs,* published in London in 1953, I wrote:

"The chief reason for my writing an account of my people is the melancholy thought that contemporary with my labours are being written the last chapters of the story of the Sikhs. By the end of the century, the Sikhs themselves will have passed into oblivion."

There was an immediate uproar among the Sikhs. "I don't wish to touch that book", Bhai Vir Singh said to someone who sought his opinion. Without having read it, Master Tara Singh also condemned it at many public meetings. After he had had a chance to go through it however, he wrote to me saying that he agreed with my prognostication of the future of the Khalsa Panth and asked me whether there was anything we could do about it.

I had many meetings with Master Tara Singh and he, along with some others including me, came to the conclusion that if we had a State in which we were in the majority, we could perhaps evolve educational curricula whereby the Sikh religion and the Khalsa tradition could be kept alive among the younger generation without violating the spirit of secularism to which the Sikhs, along with all other Indians, had committed themselves. This was, in fact, the genesis of the movement for the Punjabi Suba. The linguistic argument was only the sugar-coating for what was essentially a demand for a Sikh majority state. After prolonged agitation, the Suba was conceded and came into being in 1966. As far as I was concerned, this was all the Sikhs could have legitimately asked for in a federal democracy.

Thereafter, all chief ministers of the state were Sikhs and Sikhs were fully represented in the central cabinet; many were appointed governors of states. Two Air Chief Marshals of the Indian Air Force have been Sikhs. In 1982, Giani Zail Singh was elected President of the Republic, the first Sikh to become Head of State. Even this did not appease the Akalis.

It is a strange coincidence that about the same time as there was a revival of religious fundamentalism in the Islamic world, came the revival of aggressive Hinduism which in its turn triggered off revivalism amongst the Sikhs. In their religious zeal, Arab Sheikhs poured money into India and succeeded in persuading some untouchables in South India to convert to Islam. Orthodox Hindus were alarmed and poured in more money to counteract these moves. With the Sikhs, the challenge did not come from Islam but from Hinduism and the Sikh revivalist movement dwelt on the differences between Sikh traditions and Hindus. It started with parties of hymn singers (*raagis*) and preachers going out into Sikh villages to rekindle the spirit of Guru Gobind Singh.

Sikh fundamentalism and the minority complex added fuel to Sikh grievances. Its extreme manifestation was the proclamation in 1969 of the Sovereign Republic of Khalistan by Dr. Jagjit Singh Chauhan, once Finance Minister of the Punjab Government, then living in self-imposed exile in London. Most people regarded it as a sick Sikh joke. But the movement won supporters among Sikhs settled in England, Canada and the United States. Among the most prominent was Ganga Singh Dhillon, a prosperous businessman living in Washington D.C. Khalistan's printed passports and fake currency notes became an even sicker and bigger Sikh joke.

Both Jagjit Singh Chauhan and Ganga Singh Dhillon assumed that since I had written with enthusiasm of the Khalsa tradition, of Punjab as the homeland of the Sikhs and had supported the agitation for the Punjabi Suba, I would go along with them in their demand for Khalistan. I disabused their minds as quickly as I could. Chauhan could do no better than denounce me as a *chamcha* of the Indian government. With Dhillon I had quite an exchange of correspondence on the subject in 1981 and 1982. I had denounced his description of Sikhs as a separate nation and written that far from being discriminated against, the Sikhs enjoyed privileges far in excess of what would be warranted by their numbers (under two per cent of the population of the country). We agreed to confront each other across a table. I entered a caveat that before we engaged each other in debate we must agree on certain essential facts. I wrote to him:

"In your articles you make a large number of

assertions which are totally at variance with my reading of Sikh history... the demand for Khalistan is based on an erroneous interpretation of the word 'nation' which had an entirely different connotation when used by historians you quoted and acquired a sinister innuendo after the Muslim League demand for Pakistan. The demand is manifestly mischievous and goes against the interests of the Sikhs. It is wrong of you to dismiss the strong opposition to this demand among the Sikhs themselves as being born out of fear of the government or the Hindu majority. Nor, do for that matter, people like me oppose it to seek any favour from the government. We have the interests of the Khalsa at heart as much as you and your supporters in the States or Canada. Only we happen to be, as it were, on the scene, and you, despite your emotional attachment to your ancestral faith, live in comfort in a foreign country. For you this may be an academic exercise; for us it is hard reality."

Our correspondence became acrimonious. In my last letter to him I wrote that he should stop polluting the waters of the holy Ganga and change his name from Ganga Singh to Potomac Singh after the river which runs along Washington. I wrote:

"Dear Dhillonji,

Both you and I were compelled to leave our homes in Western Punjab because some Indian Muslims declared themselves a separate nation and established the Islamic State of Pakistan. Dhillonji, you might recall that even at that time, as there are today, Dhillon Muslims and Dhillon Hindus, who spoke the same language as you did, ate the same food and lived exactly the way you did. The only difference between

42

them and you was that you worshipped in a gurdwara while they prayed in mosques or temples. Did you then believe that the Dhillon *jats* belonged to three different nationalities?

Dhillonji, on Partition you decided to renounce your Indian nationality and settled in America. Most of us came to independent India to start a new life. You prospered as an American citizen; we prospered as citizens of free India and once again became the most prosperous community in the country. There may be some amongst us who feel they could do better and they air their grievances as citizens of a free country. But we are happy to remain Indian citizens and do not wish to suffer the same fate as Indian Muslims who clamoured for Pakistan. We feel that the logical and inevitable outcome of your propaganda of separate nationhood is a manifesto of Sikh annihilation. What kind of *guru-ka-Sikh* are you? It is ironic that while you should bear a Hindu name, Ganga Singh, you claim to belong to a separate nation and advise us Sikhs who belong to the land through which the Ganga flows to be disloyal to our motherland. I suggest that one *amrit vela* you take a dip in the icy cold waters of your neighbouring river and rechristen yourself Potomac Singh Dhillon. I remain your ex-brother Ganga-*vasi*."

Khushwant Singh

In December 1982, the self-styled President of Khalistan, Dr Jagjit Singh Chauhan, told a pressman in London that "Khalistan will be born within five years". The 54-year old doctor with a snowwhite beard like that of Santa Claus said that the moment to strike will be when Mrs Gandhi dies or is taken ill. He dismissed the

Akalis as "moderates", and an exhausted people. "I'll go and suggest that people try my cure", he proclaimed, "because I am a doctor. I have faith in the Lord, we will win."

4

The Bhindranwale
Phenomenon

To go back a little in time, the situation in the Punjab actually began to be fouled up while the Akali government under Prakash Singh Badal was in power (June 1977-February 1980). It began with a confrontation between the break-away sub-sect of the Nirankaris and followers of Jarnail Singh Bhindranwale, a non-descript youngster who had been named head of the Dam Dami Taksal, itself of marginal importance among the Sikhs. In turns, the Congress (*nokili topiwale*) and the Akalis (*neeliyaan pagganwale*) tried to exploit him by feeding his vanity. In due course, he became a formidable force and began to call the shots.

In order to understand the phenomenon of Bhindranwale, we should know something about the man and the circumstances which made it possible for a yesterday's nobody to become a somebody who could threaten the integrity and unity of a nation of over 800 million people.

Jarnail Singh was the youngest of the seven sons of a peasant farmer, Joginder Singh, a man of very modest means. He was born in 1947 in the village of Rodey (Moga district). The family was so poor that often it could not buy fodder to feed their buffalo. Jarnail Singh was able to study only upto the primary class when, in 1965 he was handed over to Sant Gurbachan Singh Khalsa, who ran a religious centre (*taksaal* or mint) in the village of Bhindran (hence Bhindranwale), known as the Dam Dami Taksaal, hallowed by its association with the last of the ten Sikh gurus, Gobind Singh. A year after joining the *taksaal,* Jarnail was married to Pritam Kaur. They had two sons.

Jarnail Singh made up for his brief schooling by an extensive study of the Sikh religious scriptures. He had an excellent memory and was soon able to quote texts when preaching sermons. On the death in a car accident on 3rd August, 1977 of Sant Kartar Singh (who had succeeded Sant Gurbachan Singh), Jarnail Singh was elected head of the Dam-Dami Taksaal. With the succession came the prefix *Sant* (Saint) and the suffix Bhindranwale, to give him the full title by which he was later known, Sant Jarnail Singh Bhindranwale.

Within a short period of becoming head of the *taksaal,* Jarnail Singh came to be recognized as the most effective instrument for the renaissance of Sikh fundamentalism. He toured villages exhorting Sikh youth to return to the spartan traditions of the Khalsa started by Guru Gobind Singh: not to clip their beards, abstain from smoking, drinking and taking drugs. Wherever, he went, he baptised young men and women by the hundreds. An integral part of his preaching was that all Sikhs should, as had been enjoined by their warrior-guru, Gobind Singh, be *shastradhari*—weapon-bearers. Besides the *kirpan* (sword), which is one of the five essential symbols of the Khalsa faith, he enjoined his followers to carry modern fire-arms like rifles and pistols. He himself always carried a revolver in a holster with a belt charged with bullets.

Jarnail Singh became important enough to be sought after by political parties. The first to try and exploit his potential as a political force during the Janata regime was Giani Zail Singh, who as leader of the Congress in the Punjab thought that with Bhindranwale's support he might be able to oust the Akalis from their stranglehold over the Sikh gurdwaras. Little did Gianiji then realize that in a few years to come, he would be hoist on his own petard.

Meanwhile the Akali party met in Anandpur and passed a resolution setting out demands of the Sikhs which could be construed as leading to Khalistan. These included the exclusive possession of Chandigarh as the Capital of the Punjab (it is to this day jointly shared by Punjab and Haryana), readjustment of the State's boundaries to incorporate Punjabi speaking areas which had been given to the neighbouring states of Himachal Pradesh and Haryana as well as a larger share of the river waters which passed through its territory. With these, the Akalis also demanded more autonomy for the state. The most controversial part of the resolution was that although the readjustment of boundaries asked for would reduce the Sikh population of Punjab to a minority, it demanded a clear statement from the government that in the re-constructed state the voice of the Sikhs would be predominant (*Khalsa ji da bol bala*).

47

The political scene blew up with the bloody confrontation between Jarnail Singh's followers and the Nirankari Sikhs at Amritsar on 13th April, 1978. The chief difference between them and orthodox Sikhs is that whereas the latter recognize only ten gurus now symbolized in the *Granth Sahib*, the Nirankaris recognize a succession of gurus. Besides worshipping a living guru (anathema to the orthodox), the Nirankaris also have two sacred texts of their own which contain passages which the orthodox regard as offensive to their gurus and the *Granth Sahib*. In November 1973, the SGPC passed a formal resolution declaring Nirankaris as renegades. Since then there have been many clashes between the orthodox Sikhs and Nirankaris, but on the Baisakhi of 1978, a procession of Sikhs including a large number of Bhindranwale's followers on their way to a Nirankari assemblage were fired upon. Thirteen were killed, including one Fauja Singh whose widow, Amarjit Kaur, later became one of the leaders of the extremists. The Nirankaris charged with murder were subsequently acquitted on the ground that they had acted in self-defence. Thereafter, there was no-let up in violence against them and their sympathizers. The head of the sect, Baba Gurbachan Singh, was slain in Delhi on 24th April, 1980. Subsequently hardly a week went by when some Nirankari or other did not fall victim to the wrath of the orthodox Khalsa.

Why these violently fundamental elements came to be aligned with the Akalis and how the Akalis managed to sustain a *morcha* and persuade upwards of 200,000 volunteers to court arrest needs to be explained. The two groups have not very much in common in their objectives. The Akalis represent the interests of the comparatively well-to-do peasant-farmers who prospered

48

with the Green Revolution. Their aim is to wrest political power from the Congress and ensure further agricultural prosperity through the liberal supply of river waters and electric power (both generated in the Punjab), as well as to set up agro-industries like sugar and textile mills to process their abundant harvests of cane and cotton. Fundamentalists who embrace Bhindranwale's followers, the *Akhand Keertani Jathas* and the Sikh Students Federation are more concerned with retaining Sikh hegemony in the Punjab by emphasizing Sikh separateness from the Hindus and making sure that the large-scale influx of Hindu agricultural labour from the states of Uttar Pradesh and Bihar, which has already reduced the Sikh proportion of Punjab's population from 56 to 52 per cent, is halted. They made common cause with the Akalis and between them cooked up a list of grievances—religious, political and economic, none of which they had bothered about when the Akali party ruled the state. The Anandpur Resolution which had been collecting dust in Akali archives for eight years, was hauled out and made into a charter of Sikh demands. Although moderate Akali leaders like Sant Longowal, G.S. Tohra and, Prakash Singh Badal attempted to water down the demands till only two substantive ones remained, viz. declaration of Chandigarh as the exclusive capital of the Punjab with a few minor readjustments of boundaries with Haryana, and reference to a Supreme Court Judge the matter of the re-allocation of river waters, the fundamentalists refused to accept anything short of permanent Sikh hegemony over an autonomous Punjab.

In 1981 things began to hot up. In February Prime Minister Indira Gandhi met the Akali leaders in Delhi and brushed off their demands as unacceptable. Akalis began mounting their offensive. The following summer there was a wave of bomb attacks, arson and killings. Extremists of the Dal Khalsa desecrated several Hindu temples by throwing heads of cows in them. In September, they hijacked an Indian Airlines plane and followed it up by an orgy of senseless killings. Their most notable victim was Lala Jagat Narain, owner of the most widely read chain of papers in the Punjab, who was murdered on 9th September.

The situation continued to deteriorate. In August 1982 the Akalis declared a holy war (*Dharm Yudh*) against the government and appointed Sant Harchand Singh Longowal as the dictator to mastermind the offensive to fill Punjab's jails. By October, almost 30,000 Akalis were behind bars. Later, they stormed the Parliament. Four policemen were slain.

There was a succession of agitations: *nahar roko, rail roko, rasta roko, kam roko* and the continuance of the *Dharam Yudh* which had little *dharma* in it with the *yudh* often descending to cowardly slayings of innocent Nirankaris and Hindus.

At last the government woke up to the very serious situation that had been created and released all Akali prisoners and invited them for a fresh round of talks. The Akalis remained adamant and insisted that the Prime Minister first accept their demands or they would carry on their agitation to disturb the Asian Games in Delhi. The government over-reacted by asking the police of Haryana, Uttar Pradesh and Delhi to prevent such demonstrations. Every Sikh travelling by rail or road to Delhi was stopped, searched and interrogated. For the first time the Sikhs were discriminated against. The unfortunate precedent set at the Asiad was invoked whenever an untoward incident involving a Sikh took place. Now the Sikh is in fact discriminated against wherever he happens to be.

I saw Bhindranwale only once in 1981 when the Akalis first launched their agitation. On that occasion his speech was largely directed against me. He had been told that I had written something about his spreading hatred between Hindus and Sikhs. He denied my allegations and explained at great length to the 30,000 strong audience that he preached the gospel of the gurus and exhorted Sikhs to return to the spartan traditions of their forefathers.

I spent a weekend listening to tapes of his speeches delivered to a succession of *jathaas* before they left the Golden Temple to offer themselves for arrest. The friend who gave them to me told me that they were available in most towns of the Punjab and eagerly listened to by Bhindranwale's innumerable admirers.

Bhindranwale usually refered to the Hindus in pejorative terminology as *topian waley* (cap-wearers), *dhotian waley* (dhoti wearers), *monay* (clean shaven) or *mahaashaas* (word used for Arya Samajists). Nirankaris were invariably referred to as *narakdhaaris*— seekers of hell. Governmental authority was described as *Hindu samraj da danda*—the stick of Hindu imperialism. Indira Gandhi was sometimes referred to as *Bibi Indra, Indra Bhain* but mostly as *Panditani* or *Panditaan di kuri*— daughter of Brahmins. Darbara (without Singh) was always spoken of as Zakaria—the Mughal governor of the Punjab who tried to exterminate the Sikhs.

Zail Singh, who was as devout a Sikh and knew as much about the Sikh scripture as Bhindranwale, was castigated for dyeing his beard and being amongst the *chappalian jhaaran waley*— dusters of sandals. And for both Zail Singh and Darbara, Bhindranwale quoted the doggerel:

'Dharam jaavey taan jaavey, Meri kursi kithey na jaavey'— *if my faith goes, I don't care, so long as I don't lose my chair.*

Bhindranwale not only preached hatred, he also preached violence. The one theme that ran through all his speeches was the need for Sikhs to be *shastradhari*—armed—not only with a *kirpan* which is understandable since it is an integral part of the Khalsa tradition, but also have firearms, with or without licences. Did the sixth guru, Hargobind, ask Emperor Jehangir for arms licences? Did Guru Gobind Singh ask Emperor Aurangzeb for them? he asked. He alleged that Hindus were allowed to keep guns without licences. He named police officers who were involved in killings, described them as drinkers of Sikh blood and exhorted his audience to punish them by finishing off their families. For the Nirankaris he had no compassion whatsoever. He lumped them with desecrators of the *Granth Sahib* who deserved to be sent to hell. The Nirankari Guru was warned that he may meet the same fate as his father.

Bhindranwale promised his audience the establishment of *Khalsa Raj*. He compared the present times with the worst days of Mughal tryanny: "If a handful of Sikhs could then triumph over the Mughals, it should not be difficult for the Sikhs to oust the government of today." He exhorted villagers to arm themselves and be ready for action when the time for action came.

If this was not preaching hatred and violence, I don't know what else it was.

Bhindranwale denied that he was a *firkaprastha*—communalist. According to him it was the *mahaashaa press* (Hindu owned newspapers) and the government which were communal and anti-Sikh. In the same breath he threatened to take the lives of 5,000 innocent Hindus if any of his followers came to harm. If this was his understanding of the teachings of the Sikh gurus then either he or I had totally missed their message. I was under the impression that the essence of Sikhism was *Sarbat da bhala*—goodwill towards all—and *na koee bairee na begaana, sagal sang hamree ban aaee* (For us there are no enemies and no strangers, all are our friends). If Bhindranwale was right, our gurus must have been wrong.

After many hours of listening to the tapes, what disturbed me most was the highly charged, hothouse atmosphere that obviously pervaded the precincts of the Golden Temple. It had no relevance to what was going on in India and the world outside. Even more disturbing was the realisation that Bhindranwale had emerged as a powerful leader and had evidently gained acceptance among a large section of Sikh youth. He spoke a language that Punjabi rustics understood and which fired his semi-literate urban followers and students. He fabricated facts to suit himself and in the fervid, hate-loaded milieu in which he held forth, no one dared to question him. His was not the voice of reason, but of unthinking passion unconcerned with the tragic consequences that engulfed his entire community and country. "It would be a sad day if the people of India and the world come to believe that Bhindranwale speaks for all Sikhs," I wrote. "He does not. And by the grace of our ten gurus and *Granth Sahib*, I hope he never will."

5

Plain Speaking on the Punjab

Bhindranwale's influence, unfortunately, continued to grow and the situation in Punjab continued to deteriorate, largely due to the passivity of the central government which shied away from talking with the Akali leaders and taking bold decisions on the issues involved. On 28th April, 1983, I made a long speech in the Rajya Sabha attempting to analyse events in the Punjab and suggesting what could be done to prevent matters from deteriorating even further. This is the text of my speech:

I would crave your indulgence for being somewhat emotional on the subject because this does concern me primarily as a Sikh, Punjabi and an Indian. Or perhaps, I should put it the other way round. It concerns me primarily as an Indian, then as a Punjabi and as a Sikh. I will try to give as objective a picture as I can of the Punjab situation as it existed yesterday and the way it has developed today.

I will try, at the same time, to draw your attention to where we have gone wrong in handling this issue and suggest some methods by which we can rectify this situation. The situation yesterday, and by that I mean a year ago, was that we were under the impression that the Akalis did not enjoy the support of the Sikh community, that the *morcha* that they had launched would peter out in a short while. We had also assumed that the Dal Khalsa and the so called National Council of Khalistan only consisted of lunatics and would be brought to heel in a very short time.

It is quite obvious that we were wrong on both these counts. The Akalis have been able to mount a *morcha* and send a lakh of people to jail and it seems that they have the capacity to continue this *morcha* indefinitely. We were also wrong in assuming that we could control the Dal Khalsa and the extremist elements. They have now not only continued to take a toll of life but have also raided armouries and thus got more arms in their hands.

The movement has expanded. That was evident from the *rasta roko morcha*. It was not restricted to the Akalis but, at their request, or at their bullying, entire villages turned out to block roads and included Hindus as well as Muslims. You will see that in the Punjabi papers. This has really assumed very serious proportions.

What action has the government taken to meet this situation?

You have outlawed the Dal Khalsa and the National Council of Khalistan. I support and welcome this move. It should have been done even earlier. But let us not get excited about threats to life. I have been on their hit list for over one year and I am here in good health standing before you. They are bluffers and bullies. We need not take them too seriously.

The more distressing thing is that the dialogue between you and the Akalis has gone on for seven or eight long months, with people shuttling between Delhi and Amritsar. Sardar Swaran Singh, the Maharaja of Patiala and various other people have been named as intermediaries. While issues have been narrowed down and practically nothing remains to be settled, discussions go on endlessly. I have yet to understand, or I am perhaps too simple-minded to understand, what exactly you are discussing and what exactly are the remaining obstacles. Why can't you get together in a room and settle them in a few hours. As Advani *ji* suggested, and he has been privy to these discussions, there is very little now to hold you back.

I would also like to enforce the point that by announcing your decisions not to the people you are negotiating with but to others was politically a wrong move and counter-productive. It showed lack of courtesy to the people with whom you were dealing. You are paying the price for it. It hurt them. They resented it and hardened their attitude towards you. It was totally unnecessary. You could have summoned them and said, "we concede these demands," which were in any event of very little consequence.

Now, I come to the situation as it exists today. Syed Shahabuddin has quite rightly pointed out that there has been bungling by the State Government in handling this issue. It seems quite obvious to all of us that either they are unwilling to handle this issue or they are unable to do so. I do not think that the state government is entirely at fault. The central government must take its share of the blame too. You have monopolised political dealings with the Akali Party and left the state government no option to deal with them except with the *danda*. The only function of the Darbara Singh government is to wield the *danda*, and you know that such treatment does not yield dividends with any people, particularly a people like the Sikhs. If you had given Darbara Singh a little more leeway and brought him into the discussions, I am sure his stature would have risen. As it is, we have a very clean chief minister though of doubtful ability as an administrator. He is totally lacking in charisma and qualities of leadership. In addition, you are depriving him of power to negotiate.

You have really put him in a very invidious situation. You saw what happened on the aftermath of the *rasta roko* agitation. A judicial inquiry was promised. Today, 20 days later, no such judicial inquiry has been started. Why?

I come to the last and the most serious incident— the murder of A.S. Atwal. It was an act of sacrilege just outside the premises of the Golden Temple. We are not still quite sure whether the shots were fired from within the Temple or whether the culprit was in the Temple or outside in the bazaar. This act has been condemned by everyone, including Sant Longowal and even Bhindranwale. I mention this specifically for the reason that unfortunately this gallant officer's name was linked with the so-called encounters in which many people have lost their lives; he was a marked man by Dal Khalsa.

You must know what Amnesty International has

had to say about encounters in this country. They are faked and are, in fact, murders. The police organise them to liquidate people whom they do not like. If this unfortunate officer's name was linked with such encounters in the popular mind, it was obvious he was a marked man.

I mention this specifically and other incidents that have taken place giving rise to the complaint that the Golden Temple has become the sanctuary for criminals. We do not have any specific evidence that this is so. It is, Mr Home Minister, your word and your government's word against the word of the Akali leaders. They deny that criminals are getting sanctuary in these temples. I know you are an honourable man. I also know they are honourable men. I have no reason to distrust them. I emphasize this point because I suspect you are trying to create a situation to provide justification for the police to enter the Golden Temple. I am with all the other members that no place of worship has any right to harbour criminals, and if it is the Golden Temple, it cannot be made an exception. But as a statesman, it is your duty to realise the volatile situation that exists in Punjab. If you want to send the police in, don't do it at this time. I know you are a wise man. I am sure you know that whatever the rights or wrongs of the situation, it will lead to a blood-bath in the Punjab.

Finally and with due humility, not being a politician, I would suggest a few steps that might be taken. It is evident that the Punjab government is unable to control the situation, and as I have said, I don't blame the Punjab government entirely. I think you have to share that blame.

Don't you think it is time to dismiss Darbara Singh and declare President's rule ?

Don't you think it is time that you entered into negotiations with the Akali party, the only party which speaks for the vast majority of Sikhs?

You have no option but to deal with the Akalis. It would be an act of statesmanship and wisdom to enter into some kind of dialogue with them. Either you will do it or these people in the Opposition will do it. If the Akalis are not allowed to share power in Punjab, there will be no peace.

Finally, when you have to tackle a thorny problem, you must not tinker with it. It is time that you grasp it boldly with a firm hand otherwise the lessons are quite clear. Today the blood-letting is confined to Punjab. If you don't come to a settlement soon, it will not remain restricted to the Punjab. There will be a reaction elsewhere. There is bound to be. If innocent people are killed in Punjab, innocent people are bound to be killed in Delhi, Haryana and elsewhere. Once that happens, Mr Home Minister, we will have history repeated. What happened in 1946 and 1947 will happen again. Neither you nor I want that. A handful of thugs will indulge in killings on that side; another handful will on this side, leading to movement and exchange of populations. God forbid if it ever takes place. It is time for you to act now.

On 8th August 1983, as the situation continued to become more alarming by the day, I addressed the Rajya Sabha again:

It would appear that we are like needles of gramophones caught in one groove. It used to be Assam. Now it is the Punjab. In the speeches of the government, the Opposition, and in fact, all of us, we have been saying the same thing over and over again for a year-and-a-half. I hope that now somebody either from the government or the Opposition will move this needle forward to something different and more positive. Quite obviously, the prime responsibility for this falls on the government. I rely on the statements of the Prime Minister, the Home Minister, the Chief Minister of Punjab and Rajiv Gandhi to make the following comments, largely to put the record straight.

The Prime Minister has gone on record to say that at different times the Akalis have been adding to their demands. To the best of my knowledge they made a concise list of 45 demands and to this day they have not added a single one to these 45. It has also been stated that the religious demands of the Akalis have been conceded. Yes, two or three very peripheral demands have been conceded. But the basic demand of an All India Gurdwara Act has been hanging fire. All the time we have been told that consultations are going on with the states. The main gurdwaras involved have agreed to this Act. I do not understand why then this is taking so much time. I know that our telephone system is very faulty. But surely it does not take a year-and-a-half to get the reactions of the states and go ahead with something which exclusively concerns the Sikh community.

Much has been said about the misuse of gurdwaras for harbouring criminals. Mr Home Minister, if you have any concrete evidence of criminals being harboured inside the Golden Temple, you should

60

place it on the Table of the House. At one time, a list
of 40 men was given to the Akali Dal. It was found
that at least four of these 40 men were not even living
in the country. They were abroad.

If you have been to the Golden Temple, as I know
you have, it has several entrances. At each of these
there are large number of armed policemen and
security officers who know by photographs and by
contact who these criminals are. How is it that in all
this time you have not been able to lay your hand on
even one of them? What kind of a government or police
are you running when a senior police officer is killed
outside the gates of the Golden Temple and his
assassin gets away in broad daylight? Is this the kind
of evidence that you are going to give us and then say
that the Golden Temple is being misused?

You have also said frequently that the Akali
leadership has been very soft towards extremists
and Khalistani elements. I concede that at one time
they were. But in recent months they have strongly
criticised and condemned all these acts of violence.
The latest reports talk of foreign interference. We all
know that when a doctor does not know what is wrong
with his patient, he invariably says that it is some
kind of viral fever. The same thing is happening here.
If we cannot get at the root of something, then we say
it is the C.I.A. Have we got any evidence of C.I.A.
interference? More recently, it was said that Pakistan
is creating Nihangs, or at least making Muslims into
Nihangs and sending them into the Punjab. Mr Home
Minister, have you caught any one of these so-called
Pakistani Nihangs? The point simply is, when you
make these insinuations about foreign agents
infiltrating the Akalis' ranks and Akalis being

influenced by them, you are insinuating treason. You are accusing Akalis of being treasonous to their country. As you well know, the record of the Akali party in patriotism and sacrifice is perhaps much better than that of your party or the Opposition parties put together.

Mr Sethi, you, more than anyone else, have got into this gramophone record groove saying "government doors are always open." Which person with self-respect who has this stigma of treason put on him, is going to enter these doors that you always talk of being kept open?

Having said all this, let me say clearly again that I have absolutely no brief for the Akalis. I feel that when they say that they condemn Khalistan, and do not support the demand, it is not enough. Words must be followed by actions. They must stop talking the language of separatism. It is time the Akalis came out more categorically in condemning separatist tendencies. They also must condemn violence in more positive terms. They must let Nirankaris off the hook because this confrontation has gone on far too long. Nirankaris have offered to expunge offensive references to Sikhism from their books. This offer should have been accepted long ago and something done to come to a settlement with them.

Basically, there are only three issues that remain to be settled. One is the readjustment of boundaries, the second the river waters dispute and the third the All India Gurdwara Act. You have offered a commission on the boundary question. I do not think this is an honest offer. It has been settled once and for all that Chandigarh must go to Punjab. It is equally clear that you cannot divide Abohar and Fazilka from Punjab for geographical and historical reasons; this is one country where you cannot have a long corridor. This settlement should be announced as soon as possible. There is also the question of giving money to Haryana. Nobody disputes that. If Punjab gets Chandigarh, Haryana must get money to build a capital of its own.

There is also the river waters question. I do not understand what we are cribbing about. You want to refer this to a river water tribunal. The Akalis have laid their cards on the table. They say 'Give it to the Supreme Court; we will accept whatever verdict it gives.'

Then, there is the All India Gurdwara Act. For some reason unknown to me and to any one else, the government seems to be dragging its feet. It is extremely painful that here on this one great problem which should unite the Opposition and the government, we are taking purely partisan attitudes. Mr. Home Minister, you must know from your secret reports about Hindu militarism. What I fear most today is the Hindu backlash. It is evident that the Sikh extremists cannot have it all their own way. If they kill innocent Hindus in the Punjab, it is only a matter of time for Hindu extremists to hit back. Then the fat will be in the fire. I know for certain in Delhi, in recent weeks, there are young Hindus going round with *trishuls* which have slogans written on them collecting money to buy arms, and saying quite clearly that if this kind of killing goes on in the Punjab, we will settle scores in Delhi and elsewhere. Once that happens whether you like it or not, you will have laid the foundations of Khalistan. For God's sake, come to a settlement now, without further delay.

ut that was not to be. By February 1984, the fat
was in the fire. For two years it smouldered, then
burst into flames that enveloped Punjab and Haryana
and threatened to spread further. For two years, the
common people of India pleaded with the Akalis and the
government to come to a settlement and save the country
from disintegration. Neither the Akalis nor the
government heeded these voices and at all times,
appeared more eager to put the other in the wrong rather
than attempting to find a just solution. It became hard
to judge which had been the more obdurate, but there
remained no doubt that if the Akalis sowed the seeds of
separatism between Sikhs and Hindus, the government
watered them till they erupted like venomous weeds
which finally threatened to choke the green wheat lands
of the two most prosperous states of India.

It was time to speak bluntly. Directly and in print,
I addressed both sides. First the Akalis:

You have been telling us that you were not seeking
power but justice for the Punjab. Why then did you
not do anything about it when you held the reins of
power in the Punjab? If it was for all Punjabis that
you sought a fairer deal, what did you do to get Punjabi
Hindus to join you? Did you not realise that by giving
your agitation a religious garb, you were deliberately
alienating the Hindus and driving a wedge between
the two sister communities? Why have you allowed a
man like Bhindranwale to go on spreading hatred
between Sikhs and Hindus from the sacred precincts
of the Temple of God—Harimandir? Were you under
any illusion that killings of innocent Hindus in the
Punjab would not rouse a Hindu backlash with
retaliatory destruction of Sikh life and property in

64

neighbouring states? You have blood on your hands. You have reduced Sikhs who till yesterday were regarded as more than first-class citizens of India into less than second-class citizens by rousing suspicions of their loyalty to their Motherland.

Next, I addressed the government:

While you were organising your lavish Asiads and NAMs and CHOGMs, did you not sense the tremors that were shaking the Punjab? Why have you not told the Akalis which of their demands are acceptable, which are not and which you are willing to submit to a commission? Does it become an administration which likes to describe itself as one that works to dither on for two long years without being able to make up its mind on simple issues? The common people of India cannot exonerate you from the charge of criminal lack of decisiveness, for the deterioration of law and order and the loss of life and property that has taken place. This chapter in our country's history has been written by your hand with an Akali pen dipped in the blood of innocents.

The extremists, meanwhile, continued to succeed in their aims. Their intentions remained very clear. Kill a few Hindus in the Punjab to provoke a Hindu backlash against the Sikhs living outside the Punjab. If sporadic killings were continued over a period of time, this would create insecurity in the minds of Hindus living in Punjab on the one side and that of Sikhs outside the Punjab on the other. In due course, they would leave their business and homes in one region to move to another where they would feel safer. This exchange of population may not have assumed the dimensions of the 1947 exodus but the pattern remained the same. If the majority of the Sikhs were compelled to migrate to the Punjab, it would in fact become Khalistan.

Did we want this to happen? I was pretty certain then, as I am now, that every patriotic Indian including 99 per cent of the Sikhs would answer No! A thousand times No! Yet we were allowing the Sikh extremists and Hindu backlashists to get away with it. I put my suggestions for a solution to various politician friends as well as wrote about them in my columns. First, let there be only one authority to handle Punjab and Haryana affairs and tell all others to keep their traps shut. I recommended imposition of martial law in both states and anywhere else where communal violence happened to break out. Second, I felt it was of utmost importance to establish liaison with the moderate Akali leadership and with its cooperation, flush out criminal elements including Bhindranwale from the Golden Temple and hit the terrorist gangs as hard as possible. On 3rd March in my column, with *Malice Towards One and All* addressing the government, I wrote: "But at the moment on no account, try to force entry into the Harimandir. A blood bath there will for ever alienate sympathies of all Sikhs and pave the way for Khalistan."

The future was to prove that my worst fears were well-founded.

On 22nd February, Sumeet Singh was murdered. Details that I learnt from members of the bereaved family had a bearing on the tragedy that was then being enacted almost daily in Punjab and Haryana.

Sumeet was one of the four sons of Navtej Singh whose father Gurbaksh Singh had set up a commune of like-minded liberals called Preetnagar between Lahore and Amritsar. He also edited the most widely read Punjabi monthly magazine, *Preetlari*. On partition of the Punjab in 1947, Preetnagar became a border town on the Indian side. After Gurbaksh Singh's death, Navtej took over the affairs of the commune as well as the editorship of *Preetlari*. And when Navtej died two years ago, Sumeet took over these responsibilities.

Like many Punjabis, this Preetnagar family was not conscious of differences between Hindus and Sikhs. Some wore long hair and beards; others did not. Sumeet had cut his hair, his brothers were *keshadharis*. Sumeet married Poonam, the daughter of the well-known trade union leader, Madan Lal Didi.

A week before his murder, Sumeet, who was in Delhi boarded a Punjab Roadways bus for Chandigarh. Near Panipat, the bus was surrounded by a Hindu mob. Since Sumeet wore a steel *kara,* he was hauled out to explain his identity. He said he was a Hindu as he did not have long hair or a beard. The leaders of the mob were not satisfied and wanted to beat him up. It was the Hindu bus driver who braved the mob and threatened to fight anyone who dared to touch Sumeet. The sacred *kara* almost cost Sumeet his life. It was a Hindu who saved it.

A week later, Sumeet, with his youngest brother Ratnikant Singh, who is *keshadhari*, decided to go to Amritsar on their scooter to do some shopping. At Lopoki they ran into an ambush by four Sikh gunmen out on a killing spree. They had already shot a couple of Hindus when they came upon the two brothers and yelled *"Ik aur shikaar mil gaya"* (we've found another game), referring obviously to the short-haired Sumeet. Ratnikant swore that Sumeet was his brother. He took off his turban and put it on Sumeet's head to show how exactly alike they looked. Sumeet held up his *kara* to show he was a Sikh. Nothing helped. The thugs shot him in the head and shoulder and left him for dead. The shots did not kill Sumeet. As he crumpled to the ground, the scooter fell on him. His brother advised him to feign death till he got help. The killers went about their bloody mission. Before running away from Lopoki, they had another look at Sumeet, and seeing that he was still alive, pumped three more shots into him. Thus these so-called Sikhs took the life of a fellow-Sikh either believing him to be a Hindu or a Sikh whose views were unpalatable to them.

The killing of Sumeet caused enormous revulsion amongst Punjabis against killer squads and their arch-patron, Bhindranwale. At Sumeet's funeral, amongst those who denounced these villains was Bibi Rajinder Kaur, Akali MP and daughter of the late Master Tara Singh. For a change, she recalled her Hindu ancestry (Masterjee was a Malhotra Hindu till the age of eleven) and named several Akali leaders whose grandparents were Hindus. An eminent Akali leader who came wearing a white turban instead of the Akali steel-blue stated openly that for once he felt ashamed of wearing the badge of his party. As the Gandhi cap, once honoured as the symbol of rectitude has today become a symbol of corruption, so the once respected steel-blue of the Akalis was becoming the symbol of all that was venal.

There was a time when the militant Khalsa had looked upon his mission in words repeated at the end of every prayer: *neotian di oat* (saviours of the helpless), *ne aasrian da aasra* (hope of those who have lost all hope), *nithavaan di thaan* (refuge for the homeless) and *nipattian di patt* (honour of those dishonoured). All this was being bartered away by a handful of blue-turbaned men to attain their selfish ends. It was significant that the last article Sumeet wrote in *Preetlari* was titled *Nahin taan bahut der ho chukee hoveygee*— Otherwise it will have become too late.

Things had come to such a pass that only the naive could have cherished the illusion that clouds would soon lift, rainbows span the heavens and skylarks sing songs of peace over the golden wheatlands of Punjab. And only fools would have believed that wounds inflicted by the people on the people with the tacit approval of their foolishly short-sighted leaders would be healed, that Punjabi Hindus and Sikhs would once again be falling into each other's arms, worshipping in each other's temples and giving their sons and daughters in marriage to each other. All that was buried in the past. The damage that had been inflicted was irreparable. The perpetrators of the Punjab tragedy would get away with their crimes with only pages of history to record their vile deeds and the ineptitude of the government.

The lapses were manifold. So were the doubts in my mind. Would criminals who spilt innocent blood be brought to trial and punished? Would people who saw them commit these crimes now be bold enough to testify against them? I doubted it. Peace bought at the price of condoning crime is always an uneasy and fragile one.

Would anyone dare to ask Akali leaders by what convolution of logic did they maintain that burning a part of the Constitution (27th February, 1984) that they had sworn to uphold in the name of God, did not amount to disrespect for it? What faith could people place on their word of honour? What guarantee was there that they would not raise new issues as they had done after the 45 demands regarding a separate personal law for the Sikhs and the amendment of Article 25? Would they aid the administration in actively nabbing criminals? Would they abjure for ever talk of separate nationhood and amend the Anandpur Sahib resolution? I doubted it. A peace bought without clarifying fundamental points of difference is no more than a truce which may be violated at will by anyone at any time.

The government on its part, deserved little credit for the way it had handled the Punjab crisis. Like the British, successive governments of free India had continued to treat it as a producer of grain and human gun fodder. On the plea that it was a border state, few industries were allowed to be set up there. Once yield from land had reached its optimum with the Green Revolution, decline set in. And with decline, disenchantment, restlessness and discord. It took Mr. M.A. Jinnah and the Muslim League almost a decade to nurture the cactus of separation on a fertile soil; it took the government and the Akalis less than three years' tillage in the most barren land to sprout the thickets of Hindu-Sikh separatism. The real job of giving Punjab more industries and finishing river projects planned many years ago to give the state and its neighbours more water and hydro-electric power fell by the wayside. The government went on talking. The people went on listening without believing a word of it.

What followed is now common knowledge. It was Bhindranwale's guns that began to do the actual talking. The Akali leaders cowed by fear into making inane statements without ever criticising him for the hateful pronouncements he was making or having the courage to tell him that a place of worship should not be used as a sanctuary for criminals or be converted into a fortress. On its part, the administration was paralysed and in full view of hundreds of armed policemen, arms continued to be smuggled into the Golden Temple complex. It could not have been very difficult for a limited commando action to capture Bhindranwale—dead or alive. At long last when the government decided to act, it did so at the worst possible time—the death anniversary of Guru Arjun when thousands of pilgrims were visiting the Temple—and in the worst manner: storming the Temple with tanks and armoured cars and blasting the Akal Takht.

Things have never been the same again. Sikhs who had nothing to do with Bhindranwale or politics felt deeply humiliated. Bhindranwale was killed which gave him a halo of martyrdom he did not deserve. It gave a fillip to the terrorist groups. Bhindranwale's ghost still stalks the Punjab countryside disturbing the sleep of the Punjabi Hindu and the conscience of the Punjabi Sikh.

6
Operation Bluestar

What actually took place on the 6th of June, 1984 at Amritsar was in fact a forcible entry made with the help of guns and tanks, resulting in a bloodbath the like of which has not been witnessed in the Golden Temple since it was built more than 380 years ago. It was an ironic coincidence of history that the tragic episode should have taken place following the anniversary homage to Arjun Dev, the fifth guru of the Sikhs, the builder of the Harimandir, compiler of the Sikh sacred scripture, the *Granth Sahib*, the first martyr of the Sikhs and the man who gave the name in which it stands, the name Amritsar—a pool of nectar.

It is unlikely that we will ever get to know the truth about how the invasion was planned and executed, the number of people killed and the damage done to the Temple. Government and Akali versions are and will forever be at variance. However, there can be little doubt that government handouts on the subject lacked credibility. Far from crushing the Khalistan movement, it had given it the sustenance it lacked and weakened the hands of Sikhs like me who were always bitterly opposed to it.

It is tempting to compare the two massacres in the history of Amritsar. The first took place 73 years ago in the neighbouring Jallianwala Bagh on 13th April, 1919. It was on Baisakhi, the day Guru Gobind Singh founded the Khalsa Panth. The recent incident followed the martyrdom anniversary of Guru Arjun Dev who could be described as the founder of the Sikh church. The figure of casualties put out by the Punjab government after the Jallianwala Bagh massacre was challenged by the committee formed by the Indian National Congress which maintained that the death toll was more than double of that put out by the government. Most historians believe that the final toll was 379 dead and over 2,000 wounded.

In the second episode, the government of the day conceded that over 300 were killed. The Akalis put the figure at well over 1,000, including women and children. The one important difference between the two events is that while General Dyer ordered his Gurkha platoon to open fire on an entirely unarmed and peaceful assembly, General Ranjit Singh Dayal (whose namesake rebuilt the Harimandir in marble and gold leaf) had his men storm the Temple complex which had been converted into a fortress and defended by desperados armed with sophisticated weapons. The one important sequel that the two episodes have is that like the Jallianwala Bagh massacre became the turning point in the history of India's freedom movement, the massacre in the Harimandir became a similar turning point in the history of the Khalistan movement.

Despite continued terrorist activity over months until the end of May 1984, the government evidently did not think that storming the Golden Temple and flushing out Bhindranwale and his supporters would put an end to the violence in the state. It was the Akali decision to step up their agitation by blocking the movement of food-grains and the possibility of increased terrorist activity that compelled the government to come to the conclusion that enough was enough. It undoubtedly felt that a surgical operation of a major dimension was necessary to prevent the cancer of violence from spreading further.

The vast majority of Indians also felt that the government had allowed matters to go from bad to worse and welcomed the decision to grasp the Bhindranwale nettle with an iron hand. If government spokesmen are to be believed, the action created a sense of relief among the general public. All the major political parties and newspapers of the country also approved of the action. The only exception to the otherwise national approval were the Sikhs. The Akalis understandably condemned this action. And no self-respecting Sikh had a kind word to say for the government or the Sikh General it deployed to carry out the Operation. The number of innocent people slain went on being increased and the desecration of the *parikrama* and the Akal Takht was magnified to leave a permanent dent in the bruised memory of the Khalsa Panth.

In short, the Sikhs began to feel isolated and a separate people. That is what the Anandpur Sahib resolution was about. What the Akalis failed to achieve by persuasion and agitation was achieved by the events of 6th June, 1984. It did not turn out to be the end of the trouble, but the beginning of bigger troubles to come. Many times, since then we have asked ourselves: Was it necessary?

The one immediate effect of the storming of the

Harimandir complex and the killings was that Mrs. Indira Gandhi deprived herself of anyone she could negotiate with on behalf of the Sikhs. In addition, the ruling Congress was no longer able to count on the support of the Sikh masses in its electoral campaign.

I predicted that the Sikh vote would go solidly to the Akali Dal. Whether or not Mrs. Gandhi and her party would be compensated by a bigger turnout of Hindu's votes in their favour remained a matter of speculation. But these were trivial matters compared to the much greater damage done to Hindu-Sikh relations. The Akalis and, more than them, Bhindranwale and his goons, did grievous harm by driving a wedge between the two communities who had always shared a common historical, linguistic and religious heritage. What the Akalis and Bhindranwale did in alienating the Hindus from the Sikhs was complemented by the governmental action in further alienating the Sikhs from the Hindus. Most uneducated Sikhs construed the desecration of their Temple as an act perpetrated by a Hindu government. In different parts of India, Sikh troops mutinied and slew their Hindu officers. Many Sikh members of Parliament and State legislatures resigned their memberships. So did one diplomat and several civil servants. Four Sikh intellectuals, including myself, handed back honours conferred on them by the government.

I wrote:

It will take a long time for the blood-stains to be washed away from the marble *parikrama* and the buildings around the Harimandir. It will take even longer for the sullen resentment smouldering in the hearts of the Sikh community to subside. Time can be the best healer, provided nothing is done to further exacerbate Sikh sentiment.

One lesson to be learnt from the storming of the Golden Temple is that it was the worst way of handling an explosive situation. Another is that political, economic and social problems are not solved by superior gunpower but by persuasion, by give-and-take.

The need of the hour is to provide a healing touch. This can best be done by acts of penance by people in power.

The point I am making can be illustrated from the two years of violence in the Punjab and the current state of lawlessness in Haryana. It is not as well-known as it should be that the single biggest contributory factor to the chain of killings in Punjab was the inability of the police to apprehend criminals and bring them to justice. Instead, the police took the easier way out by eliminating them through faked encounters. In the process, many innocent lives were lost. This alienated the sympathies of the common man from the police and at the same time roused the relatives and friends of slain innocents to seek revenge against the police. It was the kind of "wild justice" that Bacon spoke of. Since the law enforcing body itself has become privy to this kind of "wild justice", there is no escape from the vicious circle of killings and counter-killings.

The great difference between what happened (and is happening) in Punjab and what is happening in Haryana is that while in Punjab the slayings were (and are) acts of individuals or small gangs of thugs, in Haryana most of the populace has been infected with the desire to revenge what is taking place in Punjab. They will soon learn that "nothing is more costly, nothing more sterile than vengeance" (Churchill). In short, Punjabis and Haryanvis have put the entire nation on their hit lists.

7

The White Paper
& My Peace Plan

A White Paper on the Punjab Agitation was published on 10th July, 1984. I consulted over a dozen dictionaries and encyclopaedias to find why a white paper was called a white paper. I remained as blank as a piece of white paper. I found a white ant (a termite), white collar worker (a clerk), white elephant (something useless), white feather and flag (signs of defeat), a white lie and many other kinds of white things, but all they said about a White Paper was that it was "an official report from the British government on a certain subject." And went on to the next item.

Not every governmental report is a White Paper. Reports of government departments are known as Blue Books. A White Paper is only issued on a matter of unusual or international importance and has to be objective, authentic and detailed—the last word on any subject. Why colourlessness came to be attached to the doings of governments I only discovered when I read the White Paper on the Punjab agitation. It did not add anything to the little I already knew about the Akalis, Bhindranwale, the slaughter of innocents, smuggling of arms, fortifying of the Akal Takht and Operation Blue-star. Everything that this White Paper contained had appeared in our Press before. However, it was a compe-tently done job of scissors and paste. Now no one need waste hours looking through reference files or newspaper clippings: all the names and dates can be found in one slim volume—embellished with many photographs except one most people might expect to see, that of the slain Bhindranwale.

It would be unfair to describe this White Paper as a mere white washing of administrative shortcomings. On the contrary there was a candid admission of failure of intelligence at certain levels and a visible slurring over answers to crucial questions. After the Prime Minister and other state dignitaries had publicly proclaimed the existence of a foreign hand in Punjab's turmoil, the White Paper was expected to divulge its identity and produce evidence in support. It did neither. It did not tell us why the authorities first arrested Bhindranwale on charges of murder and then let him go scot-free. Nor why he was not rearrested when it was easy to do so and only reframed criminal charges when it became virtually impossible to serve a warrant of arrest on him. The most important omission was that it did not tell us why a commando action by men in plain clothes or a siege effectively cutting off food and fuel supplies was regarded impractical and a massive invasion with tanks became necessary. It did not spell out the damage caused to property other than to the Akal Takht by the cross-fire between the army and Bhindrawale's men. Most people who visited the Temple complex confirmed that the central shrine, Harimandir, had over 200 bullet marks—whether fired by Bhindranwale's men or the army no one will ever know. Nor will we ever know which of the two fired the incendiary device which destroyed the Temple archives with its irreplaceable treasure of hundreds of handwritten copies of the *Granth Sahib* and *Hukumnamahs* bearing signatures of the gurus. Why was this information suppressed?

The paper ended with posing three questions: Is it right to convert a place of worship into an arsenal? To allow it to become a hiding place for criminals? And what do we do to preserve our secular foundations from eroding? The answer to the first two questions is obviously a categorical, no never. I was then and am today equally clear about the third. Religion must be a strictly private affair. Public displays of religiosity by Presidents, Prime Ministers, Chief Ministers and other political functionaries may yield temporary electoral benefits but do irreparable harm to the country. They should be assiduously avoided.

At about the same time as this White Paper was made public, I formulated my own Peace Plan for the Punjab. It was published in many papers. This is how it ran:

1. This draft is presented for consideration of all Punjabis—Hindus, Sikhs, Muslims and Christians—as a possible means of restoring fraternal goodwill after the army is withdrawn and in the hope that the new

leadership that will emerge will keep prosperity of the state above sectarian interests. In order to do so, it is necessary to share the perspective of events of the past few months.

2. The storming of the Golden Temple on 5-6th June, 1984, despite many assurances to the contrary made in both houses of Parliament and the resultant loss of lives including hundreds of innocent men, women and children, as well as extensive damage to the Akal Takht and sacred relics housed therein, with concurrent action against most gurdwaras in the Punjab, has severely wounded the religious susceptibilities of the entire Sikh community numbering over 14 million all over the world. Punjabis of other religious communities who share this grief should come forward to help heal the wounds inflicted on the Sikhs.

3. We do not accept claims of the administration that it had no option but to storm the Temple with maximum force, never used before in a domestic operation, to capture Jarnail Singh Bhindranwale and his followers. Nor do we accept the government's version of the number of casualties, the extent of the damage caused and the quantity of arms, ammunition and narcotics allegedly discovered in the Temple. From the many contradictions in statements made by official spokesmen, it is evident that the administration intended to further tarnish the reputation of those killed in the Operation, and by inference, the reputation of the entire Sikh community. We demand that the names of those killed in the Operation should be published including the army casualty lists.

4. We call on all Punjabis to reject any attempt by government agencies to repair any part of the damaged complex of the Golden Temple and deplore the fact that

in spite of strong appeals from all sections of the Sikh community, the government has already undertaken extensive repairs. This task has traditionally been the privilege of the *Sangat* throughout Sikh history and must be achieved only through voluntary service—*kar seva*—if Sikh sentiments are to be respected.

5. Hereafter, all Punjabis should observe the 6th of June as a day of prayer for those who lost their lives on the 5th and 6th June, 1984, and in atonement for the violence done to the Golden Temple. At the same time, we must accept the fact that a section of the Sikh community shares the responsibility, along with the Akali Dal and the top Sikh religious leaders for the initial sacrilege committed at the Temple by allowing armed men to take up residence there, fortifying a part of the Temple and using it as a base for hostile action. The 6th of June should also be a day of prayer when Punjabis all over the world pledge themselves to the teaching of their gurus and the ideals preached by them.

6. Amritsar should be declared a Holy city. Sale of tobacco, liquor and meat should be forbidden within the walled city. (The status of Hardwar, Varanasi and Tirupati should be checked to make this feasible.)

7. Having gone through this traumatic experience, Sikhs must now undertake a serious introspective exercise covering all aspects of the community. This includes their status as citizens of India, of the leadership provided by different political parties, particularly the Akali Dal which has enjoyed the monopoly of being the sole "Sikh" party and so has received a large majority of Sikh votes as well as of the role and composition of the SGPC. Sikhs must evolve a new religious leadership of the Panth. Obviously serious, fundamental changes are called for. This is the time for deep, searching analysis

and an enquiry into why and how the present situation developed. Sikhs must recognise that this is a crisis affecting the entire community, both internally and vis-a-vis their future status in the country. There is need for rethinking on these subjects and cosmetic corrective measures should not be taken seriously.

8. Both existing parties, the Congress and the Akali Dal, have failed the Punjabis. While the Congress has shown no concern for the Sikh community in its hour of trial, or in honouring the assurances given by them at the time of Independence, the Akalis have exploited religious sentiments, largely to grab political power in the state and at all times to retain their hold on the SGPC at the cost of the larger interests of the community. In spelling out their demands, the Akalis failed to take the Punjabi Hindus into confidence, and so wrecked their chances of success. Had they acted as a regional party instead of as a religious one, the present situation might have been avoided. Instead, by injecting religious sentiments in essentially Punjabi demands, they pursued a path which widened the gulf between Hindus and Sikhs, thus playing the same game as the Hindu communal elements.

9. Akali connivance with Bhindranwale in allowing his followers to fortify the Akal Takht and other parts of the Golden Temple, and the reluctance of the Akali leaders to condemn the acts of terrorism perpetrated by Bindranwale's men further alienated Hindus from Sikhs and weakened the joint demands of the Punjabis. This posture also lost the sympathy of other elements in the rest of the country which otherwise might have supported Punjabi demands.

10. Contrary to democratic tradition once the two-year *morcha* had begun, the SGPC and the Akali Dal

took decisions in which they took for granted that the entire Sikh community was behind them. This was certainly not the case. To keep the *Dharam Yudh* alive (and it is debatable in whose interest this was), the Akalis let control slip out of their hands into those of extremists and gave the government the excuse to invade and desecrate the Golden Temple.

11. The general lethargy of the Sikh community, the vast majority of whom did not approve of the growing militant presence in the Golden Temple complex over the past two years, played a vital role in the tragic situation prevailing today. For all these reasons, the status quo is no longer acceptable. Either the Akali Dal must undergo a total transformation and be persuaded (or pressurised) to change its traditional *modus vivendi* or else we have to think of a political alternative. Given the massive problems of building up such a force, transformation of the Akali Dal's intrinsic character would seem the practical way.

12. In order to try to rectify the mistakes made by the Akalis, Sikhs must:

(a) Reaffirm categorically their Indian identity. They are Indians, part of India, and will oppose any proposal to establish a separate Sikh state.

(b) Amend those clauses of the Anandpur Resolution which describe Sikhs as a "separate nation" or alternatively explain that *quam* does not imply nationhood.

(c) Restate that Sikhs do not want a separate Personal Law which through its proposed provisions for succession and marriage etc. would push Sikh society back into mediaeval times and deprive Sikh women of equal rights in property, marriage and divorce given to them under the Hindu Code Bill. This would be against the Sikh principle of equality between men and women. Sikhs must also resist any attempt to amend Article 25 of the Indian Constitution which in any case recognises Sikhs as a separate religious community.

13. Through meetings of Hindus and Sikhs who share the common desire to re-establish a state of communal harmony and peace, we should work for establishing closer bonds with our Hindu brethren and through frank discussions and airing of sentiments dispel the misunderstandings which have developed and work for a close association when it comes to making major demands on behalf of the Punjab. These will include:

(a) Immediate transfer of Chandigarh to the Punjab without altering the status of Fazilka and Abohar. Minor boundary adjustments with Haryana, Himachal and Rajasthan may be made in agreement with those states or referred to a Tribunal.

(b) Settlement of the river waters dispute along the lines the Akalis and other parties had accepted earlier, giving Punjab a fair distribution of the waters. (This can be detailed according to the facts.)

14. Establishment of industrial projects and heavy industries in the Punjab. The state has a legitimate grievance that it has been deprived of adequate industrial development, that there is a lack of flour, textile and sugar mills to process the agricultural produce, that this

has led to serious discontent and educated unemployment. When the Green Revolution has attained a plateau stage, young unemployed men can no longer be absorbed on the land. The central government must grant licences for such industries without delay and plan the location of heavy industries in the state on a priority basis to achieve a balanced economy. This will help absorb the large number of unemployed youth whose disaffection has helped Bhindranwale.

15. Sikhs have always enjoyed a special position in the armed forces. However, their proportion has steadily declined from almost one third during the British rule to under 10 per cent today. This is another source of discontent, and there is fear that the present percentage may decline further with the policy of recruitment according to population proportions. Since soldiering is an integral part of the Sikh tradition as well as an important source of employment, it is imperative that the percentage of Sikhs in the armed forces should not be reduced.

Government should take measures to ensure that the 'mutinies' resulting from Sikh reaction to Operation Bluestar are considered in the perspective of the unusual circumstances of their occurrence, and do not result in a tendency to distrust the Sikhs. This would be most unfortunate as it would result in even greater alienation of the community.

I was absolutely convinced that the only way to assuage the hurt feelings of the Sikhs as well as bring the Hindu and Sikh communities closer together was to bury the past and agree to disagree on what had happened in Amritsar. The Sikhs would never see it in the same light as others. Nevertheless, I advocated that we should not allow ourselves to stew in the juices of bitterness and recrimination but from this experience, extract lessons that would help us to think more rationally in the years to come.

It was as clear as daylight to me that Punjabis had no future except as one people: Punjabis. Since almost every Punjabi politician and every political party had been discredited in the eyes of the people, there was an enormous vacuum to fill. Sikhs who had supported the Akali Dal were thoroughly disillusioned by its leaders' lack of foresight and narrow sectarian views. More than any other political party, it was the Akalis who had brought Punjab to this sorry pass. Their monopoly over Sikh politics and the stranglehold they had over gurdwara funds had to be broken. In various articles and speeches, I insisted that whatever the new leadership the Sikhs threw up, it must endeavour to take Punjabi Hindus in a fraternal embrace; whatever demands they made, whether they were for Chandigarh, readjustment of boundaries or fairer allocation of river waters, even for those which were described as purely religious, like declaring Amritsar a holy city, longer hours of relay of *Gurubani*, or an All India Gurdwara Act, they must be made jointly by Punjabi Sikhs and Hindus. Amritsar, *Gurubani* and gurdwaras are our common heritage. Likewise, Hindu communal parties should dissolve themselves and regroup only provided they have an equal number of Sikhs amongst them.

Though this appeal to *Punjabiat* might have sounded like the Punjabi version of Telugu Desam, I felt it was the only way of exorcising strife-ridden Punjab of the communal virus in its body politic and its only hope of restoring it to good health. I knew then too that it sounded like a pipe-dream but it certainly was a soothing one.

I visited Punjab in the beginning of October 1984. My hopes were belied. There were no new political parties, no new leader emerging on the horizon and the Akali Dal had, rather than losing its grip, re-established its hold over the Sikh masses. It seemed to me more than likely that as soon as its leaders were released from jail, far from being discredited, they would reassert themselves to resume their destructive roles. Once again, it would be the Anandpur Sahib Resolution, Chandigarh, River Waters, Article 25, Separate Personal Law for the Sikhs, *Dharma Yuddha morchas* and endless parleys with the central government representatives. It was clear to me that all we had done in the past few months was play Snakes and Ladders. Our dice had been swallowed by the python of violence and we were certainly back to square one.

A Punjabi proverb for the Punjab as before came to me, as I travelled around the strife-torn state:

Sehnee paindee maar
 dulattian dee
Jay kursee bahaayey
 khotian noon

If for leaders you donkeys pick.
Learn to bear the donkeys' kicks.

Little did I know then that matters were to really blow up on the last day of that month.

8

Indira Gandhi's Assassination & Its Aftermath

"For a slip made in a few seconds the price may have to be paid over many centuries," runs an Indian proverb. For an incident that took place in a few split seconds on the morning of 31st October, 1984, the entire course of Indian history took a decisive turn.

In India, October is a month of festivals. Monsoon rains are over. The summer crop of paddy has another few weeks to ripen before it is ready to be harvested. Peasants are comparatively free from their back-breaking chores. In a land where the vast majority of population is engaged in agriculture, this is the time to relax as one religious festival follows another ending with Diwali, the festival of lamps when Hindu and Sikh houses are gaily illuminated with oil lamps and fireworks are let off.

That October, festivals were on a low key because of a year of tension between Hindus and Sikhs which had often exploded in violence in the Punjab. The Sikhs were aggrieved over the storming of the Golden Temple. No Diwali lamps were lit in Sikh homes and many wore black turbans as a sign of mourning. Their anger was largely directed against Prime Minister Indira Gandhi and the Sikh President Giani Zail Singh who they believed had sanctioned the army action. Security around both had been strengthened. Mrs Gandhi's residence had three rings of security guards (numbering over 1800) on duty at all hours and the latest electronic devices to prevent intruders installed under the directions of an expert. Mrs Gandhi had been advised to wear a bullet-proof jacket when going out.

Mrs Gandhi was always very fussy about her dress and appearance. She chose her own saris and blouses to match. That morning she took particular care to wear a colourful sari and did not bother about her bullet proof vest. A television crew headed by the playwright-actor Peter Ustinov was waiting to shoot her for a BBC programme. She stepped out of her house to go into the garden to face the cameras. As she crossed through a parting in the hedge, two of her security guards, both Sikhs, opened fire on her.

"Have you heard? The Prime Minister has been shot". The voice on the phone was of a lady who had a friend working in Mrs Gandhi's household. It was 9.30 a.m. of Wednesday the 31st October 1984.

"Good Lord," I exclaimed, "who was it?"

"Sikhs, who else ? You better stay indoors for some time," she advised.

I switched on my radio to listen in to the 10 o' clock news. All India Radio announced that an attempt had been made on the life of Mrs Gandhi and that she had been seriously injured. No more. It continued with its usual programmes of song and music as well as relayed a running commentary of a cricket match between India and Pakistan being played at Islamabad. This was simply not done. When Mahatma Gandhi was assassinated 37 years ago and when Prime Ministers Jawaharlal Nehru and his successor Lal Bahadur Shastri died, All India Radio broadcast doleful religious music from the time their deaths were known till their cremations were over. It was scarcely possible that a frail, elderly woman of 67 could have survived 18 bullets pumped at close range into her. It was more likely that the announcement of her death would await the return of the President from Mauritius and her surviving son, Rajiv Gandhi, from Calcutta. Both were expected back in Delhi by the afternoon. In medieval India, deaths of ruling monarchs were not made public till a successor had been named. The practice was observed in October 1984.

In times of crises, most Indians switch on their radios to foreign broadcasts, BBC or the Voice of America. Both confirmed that Mrs Gandhi was dead and that her killers were two Sikhs of her own security guard: one had been killed on the spot, the other was severely wounded but expected to survive.

By the afternoon, crowds began to gather around the All India Institute of Medical Sciences (A.I.I.M.S.) where a team of surgeons were said to be trying desperately to save Mrs Gandhi's life. The crowds chanted *Indira Gandhi, Zindabad*—Long live Indira Gandhi. There were no Sikhs amongst them. On the contrary, it was reported that some were celebrating the event by dancing, letting off fireworks and distributing sweets. As soon as Mrs Gandhi's death was confirmed, the

Hindu's wrath against the Sikhs came to the boil. The crowds' chant changed to: *Khoon ka badla khoon say leyngey* —we will avenge blood with blood. From the A.I.I.M.S., Hindu mobs fanned out to neighbouring highways, roads and markets. Sikh-owned shops were looted and then set on fire; their owners belaboured till they fell unconscious. Cars and buses were stopped, Sikh passengers pulled out and beaten up. If the car was driven by a Sikh, petrol was taken out of its tank, sprinkled on the seats and it was set on fire. Since more than half of Delhi's taxis, trucks and privately owned buses were owned by Sikhs, by sunset thousands of them could be seen burning in different parts of the city. Even the Sikh President Zail Singh's convoy was not spared. On the way back from the A.I.I.M.S. his car was stoned, and his press officer, also a Sikh, barely managed to get away alive.

More was to come. That night, local politicians belonging to the ruling Congress party met to decide how "to teach the Sikhs a lesson they would never forget." Party cadres were mobilised. Contacts were made with lumpen elements living in shanty towns and neighbouring villages. Sikh homes and shops were marked. Trucks were commandeered; iron rods and cans of kerosene oil and petrol acquired. Rumours were floated that train-loads of Hindus massacred by Sikhs had come from the Punjab; Sikhs had poisoned Delhi's drinking water supply.

At break of dawn of 1st November, the anti-Sikh pogrom got going in right earnest. Truck-loads of hoodlums armed with steel rods, jerry cans full of kerosene oil and petrol went round the city setting fire to gurdwaras. One adjacent to my apartment was raided by a gang which threw out the carpets, the canopy and

91

awning along with the holy book, the *Granth*, in the courtyard and made a bonfire of them. They roughed up the 65-year-old priest. The gang departed, taking the gurdwara money box amid shouts of *Indira Gandhi, Zindabad.*

There was an eerie interlude of two hours befŏre the slogan shouting gang returned. This time it went for the garage of a Sikh mechanic much liked and respected by all who dealt with him. They siphoned petrol out of a car, sprinkled it on the seats, flung a lighted match in it and departed as the car went up in flames. This time the neighbours came round to douse the flames lest their own cars and homes catch fire. Once more came the eerie stillness and the evening gloom heightened by the smouldering embers of the cremated car. They came again at night. This time to set fire to a godown full of motor tyres owned by a Sikh. And again in the early hours of the morning to set fire to another car and loot Sikh shops in the neighbouring market.

Thousands of others had their long hair and beards cut off—the ultimate in humiliation for a Sikh. Hundreds of young Sikhs were doused with petrol and set alight. A more sophisticated method of killing was to fill the inside of a car tyre with petrol, light it and put the flaming garland round the neck of the victim. In outlying localities, lads from neighbouring villages descended on scattered Sikh homes, killed the men, looted everything they could find and set the rest on fire. Young women were gang-raped and some abducted. Trains and buses coming in or going out of Delhi were halted, Sikh passengers dragged out and burnt alive. Amongst the casualties were scores of army officers in uniform. There was very little resistance. In Delhi, Sikhs form a bare 7 per cent of the population. Unlike Muslims who had their separate localities, Sikhs lived amongst Hindus without the slightest feeling of insecurity. Hindus who tried to help their Sikh neighbours were threatened with violence. Nevertheless, many Sikh lives were saved by them.

Most of the looters and killers were sweepers, cobblers, day-labourers or beggars from shanty towns or villagers whose agricultural lands had been acquired to provide housing sites for Delhi's increasing population. The majority were between the ages of 12–30. Their main object was to loot radio and television sets, cycles, clocks, clothes, kitchen utensils and furniture. Bashing in Sikh skulls and seeing them burning alive were fun and games: the real object was loot. In most instances, mobs were led by members of Mrs Gandhi's Congress party including some Members of Parliament. Policemen on duty turned away their faces and took their share of the booty. Sikh houses and shops were marked for destruction in much the same ways as those of Jews in Tsarist Russia or Nazi Germany. Except a few wealthy homes in upper class residential areas defended by armed guards, no Sikh property was spared. In the heart of New Delhi's main shopping centre, Connaught Circus, Sikh-owned furniture shops were set ablaze while crowds cheered and the police looked on. There were no signs of grief over the death of their Prime Minister but plenty of envy, hate and malicious pleasure at seeing Sikhs who had done better than they being cut to size.

I awaited my turn. I felt like a partridge in a partridge shoot waiting to be flushed out of cover and shot on the wing. For the first time I realised what Jews must have felt like in Nazi Germany, what Indian Muslims must have felt like in riot-torn Bhiwandi, Jalgaon, Moradabad, Ranchi and elsewhere. For the first time I understood what words like pogrom, holocaust and genocide really meant. I was no longer a member of an over-privileged community but of one which was the object of dire hate. All day long my telephone rang. "They are burning our gurdwara, can't you do anything? They have looted our shops, can't you do anything? They have killed all Sikhs in our neighbouring *mohallas*, can't you do anything? There are scores of Sikh corpses lying along the rail track, can't you do anything?" In my turn I rang up everyone I knew from the Commissioner of Police, the Lt. Governor, the Home Minister, right up to Rashtrapati Bhavan. The only help I received was in the form of advice: "Get out of your place and hide with your Hindu friends. At least you will be able to save your life. Get out before the funeral procession starts. That is when the mobs may become violent." Impotent advice from a bunch of slow-witted men! Such things had never happened during the British rule. With the first outbreak of violence, armed police went into action. When it fired, it fired to kill. If the army was summoned, it put down riots within a few minutes with an iron hand.

But for two days there was no law or order in India's capital city nor in major cities like Kanpur, Lucknow and Bokaro. The new Prime Minister, Rajiv Gandhi, his advisers, cabinet ministers, chief ministers of states, and senior civil servants were busy receiving heads of states of foreign countries pouring into the capital to attend Mrs Gandhi's funeral. Meanwhile, Doordarshan (India's T.V.) showed nothing besides Mrs Gandhi's body lying in state with streams of mourners filing past and crowds outside chanting *Indira Gandhi Amar Rahey*—Indira Gandhi is immortal. On the second day, newspapers and the radio announced that Section 144 of the Criminal Procedure Code banning any gathering of five or more persons and night curfew had been imposed and that the police had been ordered to shoot law-breakers at sight. Nevertheless, the marauding went on merrily without anyone being shot. Ultimately, the army had to be called in. The worst killings were feared on Mrs Gandhi's funeral when large crowds returning to their homes from the site of the cremation might have another go at the hapless Sikhs. Most well-to-do Sikhs moved into hotels or took shelter in homes of their Hindu friends.

In Delhi, it took the authorities over 24 hours to realise that the police and the para-military forces were unwilling (not incapable but unwilling) to put down the rioters. Curfew was announced but never imposed; shoot at sight authorised, but never executed; extensive patrolling was more heard over All-India Radio and Doordarshan than seen with the eyes. The killing assumed the proportion of a genocide of the Sikh community.

"Get out of your place", was the repetitive advice. But go where and how? They were killing Sikhs on trains, buses, taxis, scooters.

I had half-an-hour to pack up. I wrenched off the name plate from my door. What could I take with me from my home where I had lived ever since I had been driven out of Pakistan? Ultimately, I decided to leave everything and in my overnight bag only put in the manuscript of a nearly completed novel. They could have all the rest: the two score books I had written and the few thousand I had collected, the TV set, tape recorders, clocks, watches, clothes, carpets, furniture, paintings everything. They could have the bloody lot. Thirty-seven years ago, I left the same kind of stuff to Pakistan; now I would leave it to Hindustan.

Romesh Thapar bundled us into the car of a

diplomat. We found sanctuary in the home of Rolf and Jeanne Gauffin of the Swedish Embassy. In my own homeland, I had become a refugee, deprived of my birthright to mourn the assassination of my Prime Minister. Instead, I mourned the deaths of thousands of men who were killed for no other reason than that they happened to belong to the same community as the Prime Minister's assassins.

The attendance at Mrs Gandhi's funeral was very thin because few buses plied and like the smoke of burnt buildings, a pall of fear had spread over the city. That night Rajiv Gandhi went round and with his own eyes saw the havoc that had been caused. However, at a public meeting to pay tribute to his mother, he said, "We will avenge Mrs Gandhi's death." And added after a pause, "but not in this way." His words did not inspire much confidence amongst the Sikhs. He almost explained away the general massacre as something that should have been expected: "When a big tree falls, the earth about it shakes," he said.

Nobody knows how many lives were lost in those three days following Mrs Gandhi's assassination. At first, the government put the figure at a little over 1,000, half of them in Delhi. Two months later, the official figure was raised to over 2,000 dead. Unofficial estimates put the death toll at over 6,000 for the whole of India, more than half of it in Delhi. There were over 50,000 Sikhs in a dozen or more refugee camps, amongst them over 1,300 women widowed in the previous three days.

A report entitled *Who are the Guilty?* jointly published by the Peoples' Union for Democratic Rights and the Peoples Union for Civil Liberties not only accepted the higher figure but amongst the hundred named guilty included H.K.L. Bhagat, senior member of Rajiv Gandhi's cabinet, four Members of Parliament belonging to his party and innumerable members of Delhi's Metropolitan Council as well as city fathers—all members of the ruling Congress party. Another commission of inquiry headed by a retired Chief Justice of the Supreme Court, S.M. Sikri and consisting of a panel of eminent retired civil servants including Badruddin Tyabji, Rajeshwar Dayal and Govind Narain likewise gave a damning indictment against Congress politicians, the police and Delhi Administration. Yet a third report prepared by the Citizens for Democracy was released on the 29th January, 1985 by its Chairman, retired Supreme Court Justice V.M. Tarkunde, a leading figure in the civil rights movement. It was based on extensive interviews with victims and eye-witnesses. It came to the conclusion that the "carnage was orchestrated by Congress-I" (the ruling party). According to it, although extensive violence erupted after Mrs Gandhi's death was announced, no Sikh had been killed till after plans for their massacre were matured by party leaders on the night of the 31st of October. "Clearly people's anger had not reached such an intensity as to burn a man alive and to gloat over his anguished cries or his burning flesh," it read. According to the report: "Kerosene was collected, killers were gathered from both outside and inside the localities, jhuggis (huts) and houses of Sikhs identified." The government was understandably reluctant to appoint a commission of enquiry of its own. The President's address to the two Houses of Parliament mentioned that "stern and effective measures were taken and the violence put down in the shortest possible time." It was evident that the guilty would go scot free and set a precedent that would cost the country dear. The *Sunday*, a widely circulated weekly from Calcutta, described Rajiv Gandhi's silence on the subject as "the first black mark he has got on his otherwise clean image." A senior civil servant said to me, "the tiger has tasted human blood; it was Sikh blood this time, hereafter it will be that of the well-to-do of every community." The tiger he referred to was the lumpen elements from shanty towns and deprived villages. In Parliament on 22nd January, 1985, I appealed to the government to appoint a high-powered judicial commission to go into the post-assassination violence. I was convinced that unless the guilty were identified and punished, there would be no settlement of the Punjab problem and no peace in the country. I had addressed Parliament five days earlier too—this time to pay tribute to Mrs. Gandhi. I said:

I thank you for giving me this opportunity of paying tribute to our departed leader. I speak of her in four capacities. First, as one who for a brief period had the privilege of her friendship and to whom I owe my presence in this august assembly today. Secondly, as a critic of her policies, particularly insofar as they concerned the Punjab and earned her displeasure for doing so. Thirdly, as a Sikh and a member of the same community to which her assassins belonged and bearing the stigma that many of my countrymen have imprinted on us. Finally, and above all, as an Indian who feels passionately that the most befitting tribute we can pay this great woman is to strive to achieve her unfulfilled dream of creating a united, strong, prosperous and happy India.

Mrs Gandhi's place in history is assured. No one person in the history of the world, neither dead nor living, neither male nor female, held the destinies of so many people for so long a time in their hands as did Indira Gandhi. No monarch ruled over so vast a territory inhabited by so numerous a people as diverse in race, creed, language and ways of living as did Indira Gandhi. She did not inherit an empire nor was sat upon a throne by a set of courtiers. She was put on the seat of authority by the free-will of her own people. She wore no crown save the crown of thorns that rulers often have to wear. She bore the awesome burden of office with conscientious responsibility, fortitude and cheerfulness rarely seen. I recall how in the 1979 election campaign she toured the country by plane, jeep, bullock cart and on foot non-stop and without rest or sleep for 36 hours and arrived at a social function looking as fresh, smiling and as radiantly beautiful as she always did. I know of no other woman who combined in her appearance regal dignity with feminine charm as she did and answered Hillaire Belloc's description of a beautiful woman:

> Her face was like the king's command
> When all the swords are drawn.

She took the hazards of life with unparalleled courage. And ultimately paid the price for it with her own life. As the Bard said, "She and comparisons are odious". Before her the great figures of history, the Caesars of Rome and Tsars of Russia, the Bonapartes of France and the Kaisers of Germany, the monarchs of England, the Presidents and Prime Ministers of our times pale into littleness: "She was not of this age but for all time". We will not see the likes of her in our life-times. About her we can say with conviction: she will be forever honoured, forever mourned.

Mrs Gandhi did not subscribe to any dogmas. Her one political commitment was to keep the country united. That persuasion and belief ripened into faith and that faith became a passioned intuition.

While paying my personal tribute to Mrs Gandhi, I cannot overlook mentioning the fact that her killers were men entrusted to watch over her safety. They betrayed their sacred trust because they were blinded by fanatic hate after what had happened in Amritsar in the first week of June last. They were Sikhs, the community to which I have the honour to belong. I have on several occasions described Operation Bluestar as an error of judgement and am convinced that but for that one error of judgement, we would not have had to pay so heavy a price as the loss of a Prime Minister we all loved and respected nor experienced the terrible aftermath in which thousands of innocent lives were lost. Rulers have many hard decisions to take and Mrs Gandhi must have weighed all the consequences before she made that fateful decision. However, I have not the slightest doubt in my mind that nothing would have hurt her more than to see that for a crime committed by two or more individuals their entire community would be stigmatised and punished. I fervently hope that our new rulers will honour the memory of our leader by seeing that the Sikhs are again rehabilitated as trusted and loyal citizens of their motherland.

And finally, since the nation has chosen Mrs Gandhi's son to lead the country, let me assure him that as long as he treads the right path, we will lend him our unstinted support in his endeavour to lead the country to prosperity. This is our prayer for Rajiv: "Today he puts forth the tender leaves of hope, tomorrow may he blossom and may the fruits of honour come thick upon him."

After the death of her younger son, Sanjay, in an air-accident in May 1980, Mrs Gandhi had persuaded her very reluctant elder son Rajiv to resign his job as an airline pilot to be groomed as her successor. A year before her death, she had had him elected General Secretary of her Congress party. Most ministers of cabinet, and the chief ministers of states ruled by the Congress party were nominees of Rajiv Gandhi. His succession as Prime Minister was taken for granted and announced within a few hours of her death. He realised that the best time to legitimise his nomination was the soonest possible when the sympathy wave was at its height. And the best means of gaining electoral support was by emphasising the villanous role of Sikh terrorists and their design to set up a sovereign Sikh state, Khalistan, by destroying the unity of India.

Rajiv Gandhi called the elections a month before they were due. A massive propaganda campaign was launched over the radio network (the largest in the world reaching over 90 per cent of the population), television (183 relay stations), the press and through posters. The Hindu backlash formed the central theme of the campaign. Day after day, all papers in India's 15 languages carried full page advertisements showing barbed-wire entanglements and text asking: "Will the country's border finally be moved to your doorstep?" And "Why should you feel uncomfortable riding in a taxi driven by a taxi-driver who belongs to a different state?" Huge hoardings showed two Sikhs in uniform shooting at blood-stained Mrs Gandhi against the back-drop of a map of India, or Mrs Gandhi's body lying in state with the Congress party candidate's picture doing homage to her.

The propaganda paid rich dividends. Rajiv Gandhi bagged more seats in the Parliament (401 out of 508) than ever won by his mother at the height of her popularity or his redoubtable grandfather, Pandit Nehru, at the height of his. A post-election analysis clearly indicated that four factors had contributed to the landslide in Rajiv Gandhi's favour: an anti-Sikh Hindu backlash, sympathy for the bereaved son, a splintered Opposition and the prospect of change under a young and handsome Prime Minister. Rajiv won by the largest majority gained by a sitting candidate, defeating his brother's widow, Maneka, who forfeited her security deposit. The second largest majority was gained by Rajiv's cabinet minister, H.K.L. Bhagat, in whose constituency the largest number of Sikhs had been killed.

Whatever diffidence and indecision Rajiv may have suffered from, he quickly overcame both within a short time. He had a good presence. He did not lose his temper. And even more surprising, he was able to speak better than either his mother or his grandfather. His first speech over radio and television after his mother's death was most dignified. His first broadcast to the nation after he had won the elections was equally impressive and created the impression that we had at the helm of affairs a young man who could deliver the goods—an Indian Jack Kennedy with the same kind of charm and charisma, a beautiful wife, a way with words and visions of Camelot.

Whether or not Rajiv Gandhi would be able to measure up to the enormous job of taking India out of abysmal poverty to prosperity without jeopardising its democratic structure, how he would tackle problems created by India's suicidal rate of increase of population, how he would put down the all-pervading corruption and black money when so many of his own supporters were known to be corrupt or how he would redeem his promise of giving India a clean and efficient government were then question marks. But most Indians whose opinions I solicited replied in the affirmative. "He is our best bet," said one. "If he can't do the job, no one else can," replied another. Even his critics agreed "we must give him a chance to prove himself." I decided to keep my fingers crossed.

I also made out a list of dos and don'ts for him. First, he had to restore the rule of law in the country. Of the many parts of India where lawlessness was then prevailing, Punjab should have the top priority. He should ignore politicians and political parties and talk directly to the people. He should have nothing to do with the Akalis who I felt had disgraced themselves in the eyes of the Sikh masses, for having reduced the community from opulence to beggary and from being the stoutest defenders of its integrity to people whose loyalties were suspect in the eyes of their fellow Indians. If I were Rajiv, I wrote, I would go to the Golden Temple, pay homage at the Harimandir and tell the Sikhs that the past is buried for ever, and that we must come together to restore peace in the state and bring it back on the road to greater prosperity. I assured Rajiv that were he to do this, the Sikhs would rally round him. So would the Hindus. Both communities had had enough of hate-spreading politicians and were looking for a redeemer. Rajiv could be that redeemer.

Rajiv Gandhi's Debut

Rajiv struck the right note by declaring that Punjab would get top priority. I commended him for this in a speech I made in the Rajya Sabha on 27th March, 1985, while warning that the pace being adopted was still much too slow. This is what I said:

I would like to start by commending the new government for making a very good start in dealing with the Punjab problem. The Prime Minister made a statement straightaway giving Punjab top priority. He has also set up a cabinet sub-committee. But that was in January and now we are in March. So far the only two positive achievements that one can mention are first, the release of some Akali leaders, and secondly, which I think is more important, the Prime Minister's statement at Hussainiwala spelling out certain plans for the economic recovery of the state. But you will agree that for three months, this is not very much. What distresses me more in recent months is the tone of smug self-righteousness, bordering on arrogance, which government spokesmen have adopted when they deal with the Akalis. It would appear as if all the angels are on the side of the Congress and the government, and all the devils are on the side of the Akalis. You are always ready to talk and the Akalis are unwilling to do so; you are always very sweet and reasonable but the Akalis are obstructive; you are generous, you release the Akalis, but they are ungrateful because, after having been released, they have not returned your gesture; you are patriotic, you have the weight of the country on your shoulders and they are talking of separatism. You have the government media in your hands and you have a subservient press to magnify your views and vilify the Akalis.

Unfortunately, what you project is not the truth. It is also not helpful in coming to a settlement in Punjab because all you achieve with the kind of tone that you adopt and the way you deal with them is to make them harden their attitude towards you. They are now less willing to talk to you. You have announced that the cabinet sub-committee will be visiting Punjab. If you had any foresight and statesmanship, something should have preceded this visit. You know perfectly well that when you go to Punjab, it will be only to see members of the Congress party or your cronies. The people you ought to see, and talk to will not see you. They will not talk to you because of the attitude that you have adopted.

The issues are pretty clear. We are no longer talking of the state Chandigarh should go to. We are not talking of river waters. We are not talking of holy cities and all those little footling things. We are now concerned with one major issue. It is the dignity and the self-respect of a community of 14 million people whose susceptibilities have been deeply hurt. You have to learn how to assuage those feelings and win this community back into the community that comprises India. On this you know perfectly well that the *sine qua non*, without which no dealings with the Akalis or anyone else can take place, is the institution of a high-powered judicial commission of inquiry into what happened after the assassination of the late Prime Minister. You, Mr Home Minister, have made it appear as if conceding that inquiry commission will be a great act of generosity on your part. You made it appear as if it would be a part of the package deal with the Akalis. If you have to make a package deal, it will not be with the Akalis but with the entire Sikh community.

Mr Home Minister, you must have seen that there are three reports published so far by men of the highest learning and integrity—academics respected throughout this land— men like Dr. Kothari; judges, including a retired Chief Justice of the Supreme Court and Justice Tarkunde and some others. Not one of them is a Sikh. If you have seen these reports, you will realise what a damaging indictment they have made against your administration and your party. You do not owe it to the Akalis. You do not owe it to me. You owe it to yourself and your conscience to have an impartial judicial inquiry. You must clear yourself of the calumny that has been cast in these reports. And, if you do not do so, or are not strong enough to do so, it will go down in the books of history as the biggest black mark against you.

Mr Home Minister, just a brief reference to the situation in Punjab which I had the privilege of visiting recently. You probably also have got information that power has slipped out of the hands of the Akalis, as far as the Sikh masses are concerned. It has now gone into the hands of young, thoughtless brigands who have no real backing but are a very angry lot. You might not have been told that a large number of young Sikhs today wear saffron turbans—no longer blue or white. They are wearing saffron because they have taken an oath of vengeance. What that means, I shudder to think. You are up against a community which feels unwanted, isolated, unhappy and sullen. You have to get round these people and get them on your side and free them of this atmosphere of hatred and bitterness that has been created. Although Bhindranwale is dead, his ghost haunts the Punjab countryside. I happen to be one of the Sikhs, and perhaps the only one who condemned this man when he was alive.

Now, I come to the more positive aspect of the situation. As I said, I welcome the statement the Prime Minister made at Hussainiwala. He is right in highlighting the fact that the base of the problems in Punjab are economic. Prosperity seems to be slipping out of Punjab. But economic plans are long-term measures, and the longer they take to be implemented, the longer we will have to learn to live with instability.

It is well known that the economy of Punjab is largely based on agriculture. It has been the most prosperous agricultural state of this country. It was the first to achieve the Green Revolution. But now it appears that the Green Revolution is fast approaching its plateau stage. Almost 83 per cent of the cultivable land is already under cultivation. The size of the families has increased with each generation and there is less and less land available to them. The avenues that young Sikh agriculturists had earlier of going abroad and getting jobs in England, Canada, the United States, the Middle East, etc. have closed down. They have now no future except in Punjab. At the same time, a curious thing has taken place in Punjab which many people have not noticed. It is the education explosion. Just about every little village has a school. Just about every young man is going to college. He comes out and discovers he does not know what to do. He cannot get any jobs, because there are not enough industries. He is reluctant to go back to the traditional patterns of work that his ancestors were doing. Your biggest problem is to absorb this ever-increasing number of educated young men. That can only be done if you put in massive industries in the state. If you do not do it, you, in fact, supply ready material to fundamentalists and people who believe in the use of the gun and the pistol.

I can suggest just four or five measures. I am not an economist. I really have no expertise. But it is evident even to me that Punjab needs much more water and power. We have been talking of the Thein Dam. I saw this Thein Dam under two Chief Ministers— Prakash Singh Badal and Darbara Singh. Tents were there. Labour was there. Maps were there, blueprints were there, and yet this bloody dam has not come up. If it had come up, there would have been hardly any problem of water or hydro-electric energy. Secondly, Punjab must get a much larger share of hydro-electric energy generated there. Those who come from Punjab would know that there are times in winter when the poor farmer has to get up at 2 o'clock in the morning to go and operate his tubewell because that is the only time he gets electricity. At the same time, people like us in Delhi run our air-conditioners. When we have our Republic Day, we light up all our buildings. Where does this energy come from? Mainly from Punjab and at the expense of Punjabis. In cities like Amritsar, there is load shedding of 6 or 7 hours every day. Then, we must also have many more agro-based industries. Punjab has a surplus of wheat, sugarcane and cotton but do not have enough flour, sugar or textile mills. Certainly not enough to use all the product of the state. Now that private industria-lists are reluctant to invest in Punjab, it is the duty of the state to put in state enterprises to absorb the educated, unemployed youth of the state.

Punjab is capable of maintaining a 10 per cent growth rate in industry and agriculture. It has proved it in the past, it can prove it now. If you bring back prosperity to Punjab, you can bring back peace to Punjab. The only condition is that you must have the will to do so and the honest intention to do so. Somehow, my own experience of what has happened in the past does not give me that confidence.

As events were to prove, my pessimism was uncalled for.

10

The Rajiv-Longowal Accord

On Wednesday, the 24th of July, 1985, an accord was signed between Rajiv Gandhi and Sant Harchand Singh Longowal. It was a day of victory of the forces of national integration over those plotting the country's disintegration as well as the crowning achievement of Rajiv Gandhi's nine months as Prime Minister. It was an achievement deserving of the awards of Bharat Ratnas for two men, Rajiv Gandhi and Arjun Singh, Governor of the Punjab. It is significant that in these final negotiations, several men who had played important roles in Punjab's affairs in the past were not consulted. The Prime Minister did not take the President, Cabinet Minister Buta Singh or Darbara Singh, former Chief Minister of Punjab, into confidence. Longowal's team did not include G.S. Tohra, President of the SGPC nor Prakash Singh Badal, former chief minister of the state but two lawyer-politicians, S.S.

Barnala and Balwant Singh, once Finance Minister of the state.

However, when one examined the eleven-point agreement to which Sant Longowal and Rajiv Gandhi appended their signatures on the evening of 24th July, one was tempted to ask, "Could not have all this been agreed upon before? Why did it take three years of continuous agitation and violence, which embittered relations between Hindus and Sikhs, to come to a settlement when most points of dispute had been amicably resolved at several meetings with the then Prime Minister, Mrs Indira Gandhi, and leaders of the Akali Dal ?"

The answer to these questions reflected poorly on the lack of foresight and statesmanship of Mrs Gandhi as well as the Akali leaders who came to Delhi to negotiate with her. On more than one occasion when almost every single issue had been resolved, either Mrs Gandhi or the Akalis resiled from their commitments and cast the blame for the breakdown on the other side. Mrs Gandhi was unduly obsessed with losing electoral support among Hindus of Punjab, Haryana, Himachal Pradesh, Delhi and the neighbouring states and did not want to be seen as one who knuckled under the arm-twisting tactics of the Akalis. This made her rigid in her dealings. One example of this was her award giving Chandigarh to the Punjab but making it conditional on awarding the *tehsils* of Fazilka and Abohar to Haryana. She refused to listen to the plea that Fazilka and Abohar were not contiguous to Haryana and would need a corridor through the Punjab to link them to Haryana. And corridors are provided for only among sovereign states not between states of one nation. She was equally adamant over re-opening the issue of the distribution of the waters of the Sutlej and the Beas, of which only Punjab was riparian, between Punjab, Haryana and Rajasthan. The Akalis suggested a perfectly reasonable compromise that the matter be referred to a judge of the Supreme Court and agreed that they would abide by his verdict. Mrs Gandhi insisted that if the issue was to be re-opened, it would go to the River Waters Tribunal. Such tribunals are notorious for the time they take to come to a decision. When wanting an excuse to backtrack, Mrs Gandhi relied on Bhajan Lal, Chief Minister of Haryana, the most unscrupulous and mischievous of politicians of post-independent India, to upset the apple cart. Mrs Gandhi could count on him to raise objections to any settlement with the Akalis. On one occasion, when every issue had been settled, Bhajan Bal organised anti-Sikh violence in several Haryana towns. The Akalis left the negotiating table in disgust.

On their part, the Akalis were equally shifty and showed more concern with their personal political fortunes than the welfare of the community or the country. Every few weeks, they added to their list of demands till it made an impressive total and included trivia such as re-naming a train as the Golden Temple Express and declaring Amritsar a holy city etc. Not only did they keep their *morcha* going and refrained from condemning violence let loose by Bhindranwale's goons, they alienated themselves from the Indian main-stream by burning copies of the Constitution on which they had taken oaths when they took office as chief ministers and ministers of the central or the state cabinet.

The three years between the initial launching of the so-called *Dharma Yuddha* morcha and its final termination when the accord was signed were the most tragic in the history of the Punjab since Independence.

It was a legacy of hate and vengeful shedding of blood that Rajiv Gandhi inherited from his mother. To win back the confidence of the Sikhs and restore normalcy to Punjab seemed at the time an almost impossible task.

Several factors helped Rajiv Gandhi to grasp the Punjabi nettle with determination. For one, he gained a thumping victory at the polls. The single-most important factor in his triumph was the Hindu backlash against what was portrayed as Sikh separatism. The Sikhs had been denigrated from being first class citizens of the country to less than third class and their loyalties had become suspect. The days of the proud Sardar were over and he had lost much of his swagger. At long last, Akali leaders realised the enormous damage they had done to their own community and become more amenable to reason. At the same time, Rajiv Gandhi and his advisers also sensed the peril of having a community of 14 million located on the most sensitive border of the country being in a mood of sullen rebellion. Quite rightly, they gave affairs of the Punjab top priority. Akali leaders were released, the ban on the All India Sikh Students Federation was removed, special courts were abolished, and an enquiry into the anti-Sikh violence was instituted. All these steps changed the prevailing atmosphere of despondence into one of hope. People of the Punjab, both Hindus and Sikhs, had wearied of continuing tension and prayed for the good old times to return.

Rajiv Gandhi, and perhaps more so his chief confidante, Governor Arjun Singh, played their cards with great skill. They knew that Bhajan Lal was capable of infinite mischief. Fortunately for them, serious charges of corruption had been levelled against him. Rajiv Gandhi took cognizance of these charges but decided to hold his hand till the appropriate time. Bhajan Lal saw the sword of Damocles hanging over his head. When the settlement was announced, instead of kicking up a shindig about Fazilka and Abohar as was expected of him, he meekly welcomed it as fair to Haryana.

Rajiv Gandhi also took leaders of the Opposition parties in confidence. Every negotiation with the Akalis was discussed with them and it was only after he had sensed their approval for the way he was handling the problem that he called Sant Longowal to negotiate a detailed settlement.

There is little doubt that the settlement was widely acclaimed. There were however a few snags that remained. The most important of these was the question of whether or not Sant Longowal would be able to carry the Akali party with him. The extremist faction led by Baba Joginder Singh and Jagdev Singh Talwandi had already denounced the agreement as a "sell out". So had the Sikh Students Federation. None of them counted for very much. But G.S. Tohra and Prakash Singh Badal did. Unless they lent their whole-hearted support to Longowal, there would be serious trouble. Both men aspired to be chief ministers of the state. Badal had a sort of lien on the post and I hoped he would come round to the conclusion that backing Longowal would be his best bet to regain chief ministership. Tohra was a notorious self-seeker; for 13 years he had hung on to being President of the SGPC and had had two terms as Member of Parliament during which he distinguished himself by remaining a silent spectator or being absent. Unless he was snared with the promise of a belly full of *karah parshad,* he would prove to be a sticky customer. If he were to go over to the Baba Joginder Singh camp, the Akali party would be splintered beyond repair.

Then there were the terrorists. They had been

114

largely contained, but by no means liquidated. They continued to receive arms, money and encouragement from lunatic Khalistani elements abroad as well as from individuals (not the government) in Pakistan. Although progressively more isolated, their capacity to foul the atmosphere could not be under-estimated.

As it happened, the initial euphoria over the accord did not take long to be dispelled. A month later (20th August), Sant Longowal was murdered while at prayer. He had prophesied that Sikh terrorism would end with his death (martyrdom). It did not. It was hoped that a popularly elected government would take the wind out of the sails of terrorism and easily mop up gangs that remained. In September 1985, the Akalis won a thumping victory taking 73 out of a total of 117 seats in the Punjab Assembly and formed their own one-party government with Surjit Singh Barnala as Chief Minister. But no sooner did the Akali government assume office than a faction led by ex-Chief Minister Prakash Singh Badal and backed by the formidable and wholly unscrupulous G.S. Tohra expressed their lack of confidence in the Barnala government. When the police re-entered the Golden Temple to apprehend militants who had formally proclaimed a sovereign independent State of Khalistan and hoisted Khalistani flags on the Temple's domes and minarets, the split in Akali ranks became final. Six ministers of Barnala's cabinet including Amarinder Singh of Patiala and the Speaker, Ravi Inder Singh, both wealthy men flying their own aircraft, joined Badal's dissident group. Barnala was forced to give ministerial posts and chairmanships of state-controlled public corporations to placate those that remained with him. Even so, he then had perforce to rely on the support of the Congress party to keep himself in the saddle. The dissidents were on the offensive and steadily gaining ground. Barnala was on the defensive and aware of power slowly slipping out of his hands.

Meanwhile, on an average, between three to ten innocent people continued to be murdered everyday by thugs who had no personal grudge against them. Most of the victims were Hindus, their killers largely Sikhs. Second, and fraught with more serious consequences was migration. Hindu families living in districts bordering on Pakistan were pulling out of Punjab. Those who remained received letters telling them to get out or else! Between 2,000 to 3,000 Hindus had already left their homes and shops in Punjab and sought refuge in neighbouring Haryana, Himachal or Delhi. Third was the Hindu backlash. Militant Hindu organisations like the Shiv Sena (no connection with the Bombay organisation bearing the same name) set up only two-and-a-half years before had by this time a paramilitary force of over 30,000 young men armed with sharp-pointed three-pronged *trishuls*, the emblem of Shiva, destroyer of evil. They meant to acquire firearms and out-match Sikh terrorist organisations like the Babbar Khalsa and the terrorist wing of the All India Sikh Students Federation. On 20th June, over 20,000 Shiv Sainiks paraded through the streets of Delhi shouting anti-Sikh slogans. At night, their women folk went up on their roof tops to bang their pots and pans with their rolling pins to "voice" their sympathy with Punjabi Hindu refugees. Delhi Sikhs got the message. Sikh migration from parts of India to the Punjab that had started after the widespread anti-Sikh violence following the assassination of Mrs Gandhi, picked up again. Sikhs living in Haryana were likewise made unwelcome by an agitation of the Haryana Sangharsh Samiti. Many Sikh families

living in predominantly Hindu localities began to look
for accommodation near their gurdwaras. For the first
time in the history of Delhi, which always had its Hindu
and Muslim *mohallas* (localities), Sikh *mohallas* began
to come up. One was known as Fatehgarh (Victory
Castle), close by a Sanatan Dharma Hindu temple where
some Punjabi Hindu families were given shelter. A clash
between Hindus and Sikhs was averted in the nick of
time by the police.

Northern India became like a room full of inflam-
mable gas where one untoward incident could be like a
lighted match thrown into it and cause a major explosion.
What further added to the already perilous situation
was the spirit of partisanship which had come to pervade
in the law-keeping forces. Punjabi Hindus complained
against the Punjab police which was largely Sikh. Sikhs
complained against the Central Reserve Police Force
(C.R.P.F.) and the Border Security Force (B.S.F.)
extensively deployed in the Punjab because it was largely
Hindu. They had even less faith in the Haryana and
Delhi police which had a bad record of anti-Sikh bias.

The accord was certainly in danger of being
forgotten. Its most important clauses provided for the
transfer of Chandigarh to the Punjab and compensation
in terms of land and money to Haryana. Haryana had
pinned its hopes on getting the rich cotton-growing and
predominantly Hindu and Hindi-speaking *tehsils* of
Fazilka and Abohar as well as cash to build a new capital.
The Mathew Commission appointed to settle the details
denied it these *tehsils* because of one village, Kandukhera
which voted itself Punjabi and thus rendered its *tehsils*
not contiguous to Haryana.

Justice Mathews refused to identify Hindi-speaking
areas and suggested another Commission. The transfer

of Chandigarh to Punjab scheduled for the Republic Day (26th January, 1986) was postponed. The Second Commission under Justice Venkataramiah was able to identify 45,000 acres of Hindi speaking villages and recommended yet another Commission to locate another 25,000 acres making a total of 70,000 acres as fair compensation to Haryana. The transfer of Chandigarh this time scheduled for 21st June, was postponed to 15th July. A third Commission under Justice Desai (initially given 12 hours to keep the 15th July deadline) was a non-starter as the Barnala government refused to accept its terms of reference. A fourth Commission was promised. The *Times of India* in an editorial (12th July, 1986) noted:

> . . . the Centre is at last moving away from the amateurish practice of setting artificial deadlines— "Chandigarh to be transferred by January 26", "Chandigarh to be transferred by June 21", "Chandigarh to be transferred by July 15"—only to become a prisoner of these dates.

The more important part of the accord and one which affected the future of farmers in the region was the laying of the link canal to bring waters of Punjab rivers to Haryana and Rajasthan. The Punjab government was in no hurry to dig its part of the 35 miles because of the dogged opposition of Sikh farmers. Badal denounced the deal over the river waters. Haryana had already laid its portion of the link canal and thirsty Rajasthan awaited the waters flowing in. It seemed likely that the central government would take the project out of the hands of the Punjab government to finish the task.

On 27th February, 1986, I felt compelled to address the Rajya Sabha again. Once again I condemned the growing terrorist activity and murder of innocents that took place every day. I appealed to the government to put the Akali party back in control of the Temple which was once again becoming a haven for criminals. I also repeated my plea that they should be fair to Barnala, and strengthen his hands by keeping their part of the promises made by Rajiv Gandhi. In the same breath, I called upon leaders of the Sikh community, particularly the Akali party, to come out and state categorically "Khalistan on our dead bodies." I made my own stand absolutely clear: If we have to fight a civil war, we will fight the civil war to prevent it. Those who want Khalistan, can have it in Ecuador, they can have it on the South Pole but they will not have it in India.

It was to reaffirm this sentiment that Barnala called a meeting at village Longowal, about a year later, in February 1987.

11
The Scenario in 1987-88

There comes a time in the lives of people when they find themselves at the crossroads of history—when a wrong decision taken by them can lead them along the path to ruin whereas a correct decision can ensure them continuing prosperity and fulfilment of their historic destiny. Such a moment arrived for the Sikhs in February 1987. Having overcome the initial onslaught of the High Priests, Barnala and his associates called a meeting at village Longowal. This was the moment when the Sikhs had to choose between the signpost marked Khalistan and the other marked Akhand Bharat. They certainly did not have a third choice of remaining neutral. The road marked Khalistan clearly led to an abyss which would spell disaster for the Khalsa Panth as well as for Bharat. On the other hand, the road marked Akhand Bharat would ensure them free and equal rights as citizens of the country in which they were born and for which their forefathers had fought and shed their blood. I believed that for those who decided to take the "Akhand Bharat" Highway, the meeting at village Longowal was the first important milestone. It was here that Sikhs could reaffirm their loyalty to the land of their forefathers and declare a holy war against those who had betrayed their community and country. I appealed to all Sikhs to take up the battle-cry "Longowal Chalo", to make the meeting a success and thus strengthen Barnala's hands.

It was time to refocus on the forgotten Rajiv-Longowal accord, and its objectives. State elections, the Congress connivance at an Akali victory at the polls, and the installation of an Akali government under Barnala was Rajiv Gandhi's expression of his wish to undo the errors of the past. Barnala's stoic efforts to keep the Akalis and the Sikhs in the Indian mainstream was an expression of his wish to reciprocate overtures made by the central government. In these grand designs, the exact timing of the transfer of Chandigarh to Punjab and an agreement on the division of river waters became matters of marginal importance. What mattered most was that the process of rapproachment should continue.

From the day the accord was signed, sections of Akalis had been eager to uspet the apple-cart. Although they had never seen eye to eye with each other on political matters, they ganged together to reap the harvest of stolen apples that they hoped would fall into their hands. The prime conspirator was Gurcharan Singh Tohra. With him were a motley crew of other self-seekers notably Prakash Singh Badal and Amarinder Singh. Their sole aim in coming together was to oust Barnala from power and grab it themselves. Having failed to do so legitimately through the democratic process of outvoting him in the legislature, they took to exploiting religious sentiments to gain control of the SGPC in order to misuse it to replace the Head Priests of the *takhts* and get them to issue *Hukumnamahs* and edicts against a government elected by the people.

The SGPC was set up to manage Sikh gurdwaras, not to make them into arenas for political battles. Head Priests were appointed by it to perform religious rituals and pronounce on the theological matters, not to become puppets in the hands of politicians. Neither they nor the SGPC nor any factions of the Akali party had any authority to convene assemblages of the Sarbat Khalsa or issue *Hukumnamahs* which went beyond matters of a strictly religious nature, just as they had no right to pronounce ostracism of persons for actions unrelated to the observance of the Sikh religious code. Messrs Tohra, Badal and Company broke all these hallowed traditions to achieve political predominance. They first took over the SGPC, then misused its authority to sack the High Priests and replace them with ones of their choice. They removed the security personnel employed in the Temple and allowed terrorists to regain control of the Harimandir complex.

Having consolidated their hold, they had the conclave of High Priests strike what they hoped would be a fatal blow to Barnala and his Akali Dal by ordering all Dals to dissolve themselves and merge into their United Akali Dal. The constitutents of this United Akali Dal left no one in any doubt about its aims: it was headed by the maverick police officer Simranjeet Singh Mann who had never made any secret of his support for Khalistan and included amongst others, Baba Joginder Singh, father of Bhindranwale, and Bimal Khalsa, widow of Mrs Gandhi's assassin, Beant Singh. Darshan Singh

Ragi was only an embittered mouthpiece of the supporters of Khalistan. Barnala, however, refused to walk into their trap. If they could declare him a *tankhaiya*, then the overwhelming majority of Sikhs who opposed Khalistan were *tankhaiyas* too. Never were religious institutions misused to achieve political ends as in those months.

The assemblage at village Longowal assumed importance because it gave the hitherto silent majority of Sikhs the opportunity to vocally express their loyalty to their motherland, to defy the High Priests who were mouthing their master's voices and doing their bidding and who had demeaned hallowed religious traditions and institutions. Besides reaffirming their identity with their countrymen, I appealed to the Sikhs to assemble at Longowal and unequivocally condemn the demand for Khalistan as suicide for the Sikhs, to denounce killers of innocent men, women and children as criminals and re-emphasise that gurdwaras must never give shelter to outlaws. It was time to reaffirm the principle that the police has the right to pursue fugitives from justice, whoever they may be. Longowal was the opportunity to proclaim to the world, "We are Sikhs, we are Indians and proud to be both."

Though a huge gathering assembled at Longowal, and expressed their support for Barnala, it did not give him much of a respite from the problems beseiging the state.

The Diwali of that year went uncelebrated in the Harimandir Sahib. There had been other such Diwalis as when Ahmed Shah Abdali blew it up and after Operation Bluestar. But celebrations were resumed in the years that followed. Diwali of 1987 went down in history for remaining uncelebrated for reasons other than protest against desecration: The Harimandir Sahib and many other gurdwaras had fallen into the hands of young men, none of whom had electoral legitimacy. They continued to hire and fire high priests, excommunicate people they did not like by declaring them *tankhaiyas*, make seditious speeches and hoist Khalistani flags. They summoned assemblies of the entire community which, though attended by a handful of their own types, passed resolutions in the name of the Khalsa Panth. Although few people knew their names, they had begun to matter more than the Panthic Committee, the United Akali Dal, and the Longowal (Barnala) Dals put together, because they happened to be in occupation of the sacred premises and they had guns in their hands.

Quite obviously, the gurdwaras had to be rid of these subversive elements. And more obviously, the primary responsibility for doing so rested on the Sikh community itself. The moot question remained how long it would take for the *Sangat* (congregation) to organise itself and tell these usurpers to get out and restore sanctity to its place of worship. And who would the community's new leaders be? At this critical juncture, the Sikhs found themselves without a leader who commanded respect and who could give them guidance. Such a leader had to be either totally free of party affiliations such as Sants and Babas are. Or an Akali. Though there were many Sants and Babas held in esteem by the masses, none had come forward to shoulder this responsibility. They would undertake *Kar Sewa* to cleanse sacred pools or repair crumbling edifices but did not dare to take the broom to sweep away human filth. Sikh members of the Congress or Communist parties abstained, from taking interest in gurdwara affairs. That left the field to the Akalis, split at the time into factions and sub-factions.

It did not really matter very much who would emerge

as the new leader. Whoever he was, I was sure he was bound to be an embittered man, owing his position to men even more embittered than himself. This was the scenario the government would have to face when it decided to end President's rule in the state. It would have to call elections to the SGPC and follow them up with fresh elections to the Vidhan Sabha. This would give some idea of the mood of the Khalsa Panth and also that of other Punjabis. Only then could plans for the future of the state be made. Equally important, I strongly felt that it was about time the central government came clean about its intentions regarding the Rajiv-Longowal accord. There had already been enough procrastinating over fulfilling its terms and fooling of the public by setting up commissions to determine this or that. Punjabis had begun to suspect that the government did not mean to honour its commitments.

Among other things, once again I urged the government to step up the pace of industrialisation in the Punjab to provide employment to the increasing number of young men coming out of schools and colleges. Till that time I suggested that they should be recruited in massive numbers into the police and para-military organisations and be posted out of Punjab for training and earlier years of service. It was essential, I felt, that Punjabi, particularly Sikh youth, should be exposed to the comparatively less communally poisoned air to get a national perspective instead of being allowed to stew in their own juices and be tempted to take to the path of terrorism.

In May 1988, I raised my glass to Governor Siddhartha Shankar Ray. We had just heard the news that the Golden Temple complex had been cleared of terrorists.

My companions were two distinguished retired Generals, one a Hindu, the other a Sikh. They responded by raising their glasses but not with much enthusiasm.

"I am not sure if there is very much to celebrate," said the Hindu General, "we must wait till we know how the Sikh masses will react. Will they regard it as a liberation of their Temple from clutches of killers or yet another Operation Bluestar?"

"This was no Bluestar," said the Sikh General. "As a matter of fact, it has shown that this kind of job is better done by the police than the army. Without stepping into the Temple, they got most of their men alive. No blasting of sacred buildings by tanks. That is why there was no uprising of the Sikh peasantry or desertions from the army. I only fear that the Akali leaders will try to make it into another Bluestar. They have no scruples." I agreed. No politicians had scruples, least of all the Akalis. While the terrorists had been in control, not one of them, neither Akali nor Congressmen had dared to go near the Temple. Now that the Temple had been cleared, the Akalis would cry themselves hoarse accusing the government of desecrating the Temple while the Congressmen would claim a victory without having the courage to follow it up by helping to clean it up and restore its religious *maryada* (ritual). The greatest danger was that while most Sikhs agreed that the Temple needed being cleared of terrorists, and the police rendered signal service to the community, they also felt the community had been humiliated. The Doordarshan coverage showing men being shot and others walking dejectedly with their hands raised above their heads damaged their self-image and esteem. A Sikh, even though a murderer, must never surrender. Even Bhindranwale had fought to the last.

I feared that although there was little sympathy

with these killers, the feeling of having been humiliated could be turned into anger against the humiliators. The government claim that police action had broken the backs of terrorist organisations was not tenable. The massacre of over forty hapless workers from Bihar and Orissa on the Sutlej-Yamuna link canal and bomb explosions in Haryana and Himachal had shown that there was a reservoir from which terrorists continued to draw new recruits. A Penta, Manochal or Brahma would inevitably be replaced by equally ruthless killers unless the reservoir of hate was drained to the dregs. The argument went on late into the night. The euphoria created by the successful execution of a delicate mission was dampened by the prospect of politicians making capital out of it. On two points all three of us were agreed. One, that the police action should not become a precedent and flushing out of criminals from places of worship should be left to worshippers' organisations. Two, that the relevant laws should specifically require of those entrusted with the management of the shrines that places of worship do not become sanctuaries for killers on the run. Once the doors of gurdwaras were barred against terrorists and peasants refused to give them shelter, they would have no place to hide except a few sparsely covered jungles or tall-growing crops, both of which could be easily combed by the police.

Siddhartha Shankar Ray was the author of the epigram, "He who controls the Golden Temple controls the Punjab." It so happened that in May 1988, he controlled both the Temple and the state. He was assured of the unquestionable control of the state as long as President's rule lasted. The same could not be said about his control over the Golden Temple complex. He would have to relinquish it, the sooner the better. He knew

Khushwant Singh

well that the longer the police controlled the ingress of worshippers, made them pass through metal detectors and frisked them, the stronger the resentment against governmental interference would grow. There could be no genuine restoration of *maryada* unless worshippers had free access to the Temple and unless it was carried out by *granthis* and *raagis* empowered by the congregation and not nominees of the government. No Buta Singhs or Nihang Santa Singhs could meddle in the affairs of the Harimandir or the Akal Takht. The only legitimate safeguard, and that also after obtaining permission of the head *granthis* and the *Jathedar* of the Akal Takht could be to provide that no one would be allowed in with any weapon save the *kirpans* authorised by religious traditions. Carrying of firearms into the Temple had to be banned forever.

Ray's immediate problem was to find some independent organisation to take over the management of the Temple. His options were limited. The SGPC was in shambles. Ever since G S Tohra abdicated his authority by letting in Bhindranwale and his killer squads, the head priests or leaders of different terrorist factions had been calling the shots. The government could not afford to take the chance of restoring control to the SGPC, still presided over by G S Tohra, even though he was behind bars. It could not even afford to have fresh elections to the SGPC immediately. In the past 16 years that Tohra had been president, he had put his men in command of vote-banks and would undoubtedly be re-elected for the 17th time.

The other alternatives were Jasbir Singh Rode and Darshan Singh Ragi. The government build-up of Rode remained an enigma. Here was a man closely related to Bhindranwale and a member of the Damdami Taksal.

He had a criminal record and his support for Khalistan was unqualified. After years of pursuing him, the government had succeeded in getting him extradited. He was brought back in handcuffs and lodged in Jodhpur Jail. One fine morning he was released and allowed to be appointed Head Priest of the Akal Takht. Whose brainchild was Rode? Neither Buta Singh's nor Ray's. It was Sushil Muni who lives in the United States who persuaded one of Rajiv Gandhi's counsellors to release Rode and through him, open a dialogue with the terrorists. The experiment proved to be a disastrous failure. When released from jail, Rode emerged a powerful and dangerous element in Sikh politics. Wherever he went, he drew large audiences. I feared that he would become another Bhindranwale created, like his predecessor was created, by the Congress Party and the government.

The only Sikh to match Rode in communal esteem was Darshan Singh Ragi. Now that the terrorists had been cleared from the Temple complex, I felt Ragi could be persuaded to return to it. By now, he might also have learnt that he was a much better *Raagi* than he was a politician and could be persuaded to stick to hymn-singing and service of the Harimandir as the head of an organisation to replace the almost defunct SGPC. He was the only man who was acceptable to the Sikhs as well as the administration.

The Akali Party was in total disarray. Numerically, the more important was the Unified Akali Dal headed by Amarinder Singh. But I did not see Amarinder Singh being able to outmanoeuvre his chief rival in the past, Prakash Singh Badal. Amarinder Singh was suspected of being a government stooge, keener on becoming chief minister than leading his party in times of political turmoil. Badal, when he was released from jail after Operation Bluestar, had had everything going for him: the heroic image of a man who had suffered imprisonment several times including during the Emergency. He had twice been chief minister, commanding the confidence of the Punjabi-Hindus as well as the Jat Sikh peasantry. He had had all the aces, kings and queens in the hand served out to him. If he had played them with skill, he would have had no difficulty in being recognised as the leader by both the people and the government. But in his anxiety to earn popularity with the Sikhs, he took to praising terrorists and accusing the government of organising fake encounters. Bhindranwale had openly expressed contempt for Badal. Badal's attempt to get on Rode's bandwagon earned him more contempt and also forfeited the confidence Punjabi Hindus had placed in him. He threw away all his trump cards to become a joker himself.

Little remained of the Longowal faction of the Akali Party. Not one of them could be reckoned on for more than being able to win his seat in the next election. Barnala had lost out by being a gentleman in a gang of thieves and by being too weak to stand up against the central government when it failed to fulfill the terms of the Rajiv-Longowal accord. Balwant Singh, because of his caste (he was not a Jat) and the very little respect he commanded for being crafty, was never likely to go further than being Man Friday to any chief minister. The rising star in Barnala's group, Premsingh Chandumajra, had blotted his book by harbouring terrorists and exposing himself to charges of extensive corruption during his short term as minister.

There were other reasons why for electoral purposes the Longowal group had ceased to count. The stuff these men were made of was clearly exposed during the ten days that "Operation Flush Out" lasted. None of them had dared to go to Amritsar while Rode ruled the roost. Their brave words were solely addressed to the government and for public consumption. They wanted to appear to be doing something for the Panth. They made sure that press photographers were around when they were "battling" with the police. At the same time, they were ringing up police officials and pleading that they should not be put in Chandigarh jail because it had too many terrorists who might do violence to them. Besides, Chandigarh jail had no facilities like fans and air-conditioned rooms. They were allowed to make angry speeches, be garlanded by their cronies and photographed making mock defiance of the police. Then they were driven to the state guest house where several air-conditioned rooms had been declared jails. Of such men had Akbar Illahabadi spoken:

Quam kay gham mein dinner khaatey hain hukkam kay saath.
Ranj leader ko bahut hain, magar qaraam kay saath.

In the affliction of the community, they dine with their rulers.
Our leader is full of commisseration but likes it with comfort.

What respect could the masses have for clowns like these?
The first priority thus was to reorganise the management of the Golden Temple and other gurdwaras. Till a new Act was passed to supersede the Gurdwara Act of 1925, this could be done by an ordinance which

Singh

provided the association of respected Sikhs not tainted by their closeness to the government. The second priority was to stamp out terrorism. Though in the recent past, its incidence had been horrendous, I believed that the cleaning up of the Harimandir would show that its back had been broken. Third, I felt that President's rule should not be extended and Punjab should go to the polls as soon as possible. I was sure the old leaders would be swept aside and hopefully, a new breed of men would take their place. It was for Rajiv Gandhi to make the long overdue gesture of friendship that the Sikhs had been waiting for: sack ministers whose names were connected with the holocaust of November 1984 and go to the Harimandir to reclaim the affection of the Khalsa Panth.

Rajiv Gandhi did neither, though he, the Governor of the Punjab and his adviser told us that the situation in the Punjab was fast returning to normal. Terrorism was being contained and would soon become a memory of the past. They gave us statistics which reassured us. At the same time, Akali leaders told us that the situation was getting worse, the number of killings was on the rise and terrorism would soon become beyond the control of the para-military forces. They gave us figures which were totally at variance with those issued by the government. It was difficult to decide whom to believe.

12
Punjab Diary 1989-1992

In the last few years, I have got into the habit of keeping a diary on events in the Punjab. Some of the pages are reprinted here. They record ups and downs in the scenario, and my own corresponding swings in mood—often hopeful, more often despondent.

May 1989

I have a Sikh friend in Delhi who drove across the Punjab to immerse his mother's ashes in a stream near their ancestral village which is the Mand area, said to be the most terrorist-infested in the state. Like most Sikhs, this friend was very agitated over Operation Bluestar. After having lived through the November 1984 anti-Sikh violence, he seriously thought of migrating to the United States. He did not believe a word of the government's propaganda about the Punjab, and readily lent his ear to what was spread by the Akalis: that most young Sikhs had fled the Punjab or were in jail and that the Hindus meant to wipe out the Sikh community because they hated Sikhs. I did not really expect to get an objective assessment of the situation from him.

He spent quite some time in the Mand driving about freely without being harassed by the police. He visited schools and colleges where attendance was full. He was pleasantly surprised to see that the area which had been submerged under floods last year was under cultivation. "Every inch of it," he said. "I will not be surprised if they break all previous harvest records," he added. The one thing that struck him as odd was the number of new and large gurdwaras that have come up in every village. "They switch on their loudspeakers in the early hours of the morning. All the prayers and the *Keertans* are taped. The *granthis* simply press the button and go back to sleep. "I don't understand this phenomenon," he said.

Neither do I.

I assured him that temples, mosques and churches are mushrooming all over the country. It would be erroneous to deduce that this means a massive religious revival. Places of worship have become commercial institutions from which people with vested interests draw handsome dividends. The control of a gurdwara is more profitable than owning a cinema, a petrol station or a gas agency. And free of tax.

"Things are not as bad in the Punjab as they have been painted," he said. "We living outside the Punjab believe garbled stories of how grim the situation is. Sikhs living in the Punjab think we who live outside the Punjab are having a rough time. Wherever I stopped, people noticed my Delhi number plate and made anxious enquiries about Sikhs living in other states." He confirmed my gut feeling that at long last Punjab is on the mend. Give it a few more months of freedom from agitations, *morchas* and politicians and we will see the end of terrorism and return to peace and prosperity. Amen!

June 1989

From the Punjab comes both good and bad news. First, the bad. Khalistani terrorists have picked up yet another target in their nefarious designs to divide Hindu from Sikh by concentrating their fire on the *Hind Samachar* group of papers published from Jalandhar and Delhi. That is not new because they have already killed the founder Lala Jagat Narain and his son Ramesh Chandra as well as some reporters. Now they have trained their guns on poor hawkers who distribute their papers. They are soft targets because they are unprotected: they do not have political bias; most of them can't even read the papers they hawk. Selling papers provides them and their families their *dal-roti*. Killing them is not going to kill the *Hind Samachar*. On the contrary, in all likelihood, more people would want to know what is it in the publications that the terrorists want to prevent their reading them. Their circulation, already much the highest in the region, is likely to thus go up higher.

The *Hind Samachar* group is accused of having an anti-Sikh bias. This is not true. They have an anti-Akali bias—which is altogether a different matter. I have had many differences with them. I think they were wrong in asking Punjabi Hindus to declare Hindi as their mother

135

tongue, opposing the Punjabi Suba and supporting Operation Bluestar. However, since they felt they were right, they had every right to say so. That is what freedom of the Press is all about. At the same time, they carried everything I wrote on the language problem, the Suba movement and Bluestar without changing a single comma. Pressure was brought on them to drop my column, but they refused to give in. They regularly carry long, eulogistic articles on the Sikh Gurus and Sikhism. Next to *Ajit, The Hind Samachar* papers are the most widely read by the Sikhs. I hope they will not give in to this murderous blackmail.

Now the good news. In two different villages in the Punjab, gangs of terrorists were taken on by the villagers themselves without the police being anywhere in sight. And in both, the villagers beat their would-be killers to death. That's the kind of guts villagers have to show to rid themselves of this menace to civilised living.

And the best news of all was of the two young Sikhs who laid down their lives and prevented a massacre of Hindu fellow passengers travelling in the same bus. This was true heroism and the kind of martyrdom the Gurus would have blessed. Their names will be honoured for years to come. Meer Anees's lines are apt:

*Sab hain Waheed-i-asr yeh ghul
    chaar soo utthey
Duniya mein jo Shaheed utthey
    surkhroo utthey*

All of them are unique in all times,
Let this be bruited in all lands
Wherever in the world men rise to
lay down their lives for a cause,
They rise again covered with glory.

December 1989

Punjab has a new Governar, Nirmal Mukherji and the country a new Government. Once again, I am hopeful of a fresh approach to the Punjab imbroglio as the Janata Dal plan to restore peace in the Punjab begins to unfold itself. The Prime Minister's visit to the Golden Temple accompanied by Chaudhari Devi Lal whom I regard as the kingpin of the exercise and I.K. Gujral who commands the respect and affection of both Punjabi Hindus and Sikhs is the first major step towards erasing the bitter memories of the desecration of the Temple during Operation Bluestar. It should create the right atmosphere for a dialogue. But we must not fool ourselves into believing that thereafter it will be plain sailing. Many stormy situations will erupt and unless the administration is quite clear in its objectives and the means to achieve them, its boat will be rocked and may flounder.

I hope they will state in categorical terms who they will talk to and who they will not talk to. It is best to eliminate those with whom they will have no dialogue: those who carry guns in their hands and those who support Khalistan have no right to sit at the negotiating table till they give up their weapons and their demand of a separate state which entails dismemberment of the country. Will they ask Simranjeet Singh Mann who has emerged as the top Akali leader what exactly he stands for before they open a dialogue with him? He cannot have both Khalistan and take an oath on the Constitution to maintain the integrity of the country. What does he mean when he says that he stands by the ideals of Bhindranwale. Did Bhindranwale support Khalistan ? He did not say so in clear words but he did so by implication. He stood for Hindu-Sikh separatism. In fact,

137

he said many hateful things about the Hindus to the extent of eliminating Hindu presence from the Punjab. It is the same with the Anandpur Sahib Resolution. Portions of it which can be construed as demands for a separate state must be amended before it is put on the negotiating table.

The most thorny problem will be to find the person or persons who will speak for the Punjab. Neither Simranjeet Singh Mann nor Badal, Tohra nor Talwandi will do: they represent only different factions of the Akalis. Not all Sikhs are Akalis and no Punjabi Hindu subscribes to their communal ideology. Let there be fresh elections to the Punjab Assembly so that we know who the real leaders are. But only after the citizens are assured that they can exercise their franchise freely and without fear. They were not able to do so in the recent Lok Sabha elections, as is clearly evident from the winners. For the first time Punjab which is predominantly Jat is not represented by Jats but men and women victims of police oppression or associated with those charged with conspiring to assassinate Mrs Gandhi and hijacking of an Indian Airlines plane. In any negotiation the voice of the Punjabi Hindus must be heard alongside those of Punjabi Sikhs.

The Longowal-Rajiv Gandhi accord was murdered by Rajiv Gandhi. A new accord along the same lines can be easily re-drawn. Matters which concern both Punjab and Haryana must be, and can be, sorted out between the chief ministers of the two states. It is here that Chaudhary Devi Lal can play a decisive role of a peacemaker. He was able to come to a settlement with Badal. He can come to one now.

June 1990

Over the last three years I have been maintaining that terrorists in Punjab are no longer motivated by religious or political zeal but are simply gangs of dacoits after loot, peddling smuggled narcotics, abducting the well-to-do and extorting money from their relatives, settling family vendettas or murdering people they suspect of being informers. No matter how they style themselves—Bhindranwale Tiger Force, Khalsa Liberation Army—or whatever, most of them are neither Khalsa (many have clipped beards) nor excited by Khalistan. How else can we explain the cold blooded murders of old women and children? No Akali leader, be it Simranjeet Singh Mann, Tohra, Talwandi or Badal has any hold over them. On the contrary, they dare not say anything against them lest they incur their wrath. Give them what they want: Chandigarh, all the river waters, boundary adjustments to their hearts' desire and it will make no difference. The only answer to thuggery is Rebeiro's bullet but with the necessary addition that the terrorist's bullets must be met by bullets fired in self-defence by the people themselves. Neither the police nor the para-military forces will succeed in wiping them out unless the common peasantry joins in the crusade. Police behaviour has in the past been counter-productive. It is common knowledge that many police posts in the worst-affected areas are locked from the inside at night leaving farmers at the mercy of terrorist gangs. And when farmers in fear of their lives give shelter or food to terrorists the police vents its ire on them. The administration must arm farmers and let them defend their own villages against marauders. This has been done with success in several villages in the most terrorist affected areas.

139

I was heartened to see this aspect of counter-terrorism in a film aptly entitled *Kabahoon na chhadai kheyd*—never yield the battle field—taken from Guru Gobind Singh's famous invocation to Shiva to grant him victory. For the first time, Doordarshan portrayed interviews taken by Rajiv K. Bajaj of *Surya* showing village men and women defending their homes with old muskets and ·303 rifles of World War I vintage. Some of it was undoubtedly bravado put up for the filming. Nevertheless, the message came through clearly. Don't rely entirely on the police to protect you. Fight your own battles. Your cause is just and the great Guru will grant you victory.

I for one am not too impressed by the charge of killing in faked encounters. I have little doubt that some encounters are faked to get rid of thugs against whom it would be impossible to get anyone to give evidence in court. Avoiding court procedures, however reprehensible in a civilised society, can be justified in a war situation of the kind that prevails in certain areas of the Punjab. Almost all of the men killed in these encounters, faked or real, have criminal records and prices on their heads. It has become a war of attrition and has to be fought according to its own rules.

August 1990

Virendra Verma, Governor of Punjab, has been telling Punjabis that Operation Bluestar was a blunder. So did his predecessor Nirmal Mukherji during the short term he ruled the state. It can be assumed that both Governors had the approval of the National Front Government to make these statements. And that they were not made only to appease Sikh sentiment but to put the record straight for all Indians. Their predecessor, Siddhartha Shankar Ray, also admitted in private conversation that the root cause of continuing terrorism in the state was the storming of the Golden Temple by the army and the unpunished anti-Sikh violence perpetrated with the active connivance of the Congress (I) leaders. So in the cacophony of confusing opinions, we have at least arrived at a consensus on the diagnosis of the sickness that has afflicted the Punjab.

When I lodged my formal protest against Bluestar by returning the Padma Bhushan conferred on me, I was roundly condemned as a Sikh communalist. I was flooded with abusive letters, telegrams and phone calls. The fact that I had also condemned Bhindranwale and was threatened with elimination by his followers was conveniently forgotten. Now I feel vindicated. I would feel happier if it is recognised that what I did, wrote and spoke was not as a Sikh but as an Indian.

More strongly than ever before, I feel that the White Paper on the Punjab Agitation issued by Mrs Gandhi's government and endorsed by the two Houses of Parliament should be suitably amended or put in a garbage bin. The first part detailing the sequence of Akali *morchas*, the anti-Hindu tirades of Bhindranwale and the violence triggered off by them are matters of historical fact which cannot be controverted. It is time we admitted that what is missing from these pages is the government's own connivance in the building up of Bhindranwale, allowing arms to be smuggled into the Temple complex and backtracking from settlements with the Akali leaders after agreeing on all points. (The Longowal-Rajiv Gandhi accord was almost entirely based on these earlier settlements). What is largely fabrication is the sequence of the armed confrontation between Bhindranwale's well-entrenched followers and the invading army, the casualties on either side, the loss of innocent lives and the damage done to sacred property. It is now abundantly clear that the army botched up the operation, the death toll on either side (and of pilgrims caught in the crossfire) was much heavier than mentioned in the White Paper. The destruction of the Akal Takht, the entrance to the central shrine and the archives remains as shrouded in black silence as the names of men, women and children who lost their lives in the encounter. How, in full knowledge of all this, President Zail Singh was persuaded (or coerced) into decorating officers and men who took part in the Operation with awards for gallantry, boggles the imagination. The most convincing argument against Operation Bluestar was Operation Black Thunder carried out by marksmen. There was no damage to sacred property and the loss of life was minimal—only two killed. No offence was caused to Sikh sentiment.

One major undertaking given by the National Front Government remains unfulfilled. And seeing the little it has done in that direction in the seven months it has been in power seems likely to remain unfulfilled—this is regarding the punishment to be meted out to perpetrators of the anti-Sikh pogrom in November 1984. Why is it dragging its feet on what was undoubtedly the vilest deed in the history of India since Independence?

We must learn to look upon such events not as Hindus, Muslims, Christians or Sikhs but as Indians. Bhindranwale was an evil man; the Akalis were dishonest in inflating their demands, "Bluestar" was a Himalayan blunder, "Black Thunder" was not; the killings of innocents in 1984 was diabolic; the reluctance to punish criminals who perpetrated it is a continuing crime.

December 1990

It grieves me to note that our protest against the code of conduct for the media dictated by the so called Panthic Committee (no one knows how many there are) has claimed its first victim in the cold-blooded murder of Rajender Kumar Talib, Station Director of All India Radio in Chandigarh. He was only doing his duty and had nothing whatsoever to do with the discussion that had been recorded earlier by the Delhi Radio Station between S. Sahay, ex-Delhi Editor of *The Statesman*, the retired Director General of AIR and Doordarshan and myself with C.S. Pandit acting as the moderator. All we said was that no one had the moral right to tell the media what it should or should not say—neither the government, nor proprietors of papers nor the public. Media people worth their salt have their own personal codes of conduct of which the most important is that they must never give in to pressure of money or power, nor knuckle under threats of violence. This so-called Panthic Committee had issued a diktat which required us, amongst other things, to use the honorofic Sant before the name of Bhindranwale and describe terrorists as freedom fighters for Khalistan. I remember when I was Editor of *The Hindustan Times* ,I had issued instructions that the title Sant was never to be used with the name of Bhindranwale.

Bhindranwale was then alive. I have never used the title nor have any intention of using it in the future. As for the Panthic Committee's freedom fighters, I described them as *looteyrey* (robbers) because that is exactly what I think they are: killers of innocent men, women and children, abductors and rapists, living on extortion and smuggling of narcotics. It can be held against me that I am bold enough to say all this because I live in comparative security provided to me in the

143

Capital. What about media persons in Punjab who are exposed to these gunmen all the time and have already lost over 150 of their colleagues to the killers? There is little people like me can do for them except express our sympathy and solidarity. It is for the government to provide them better security so that they can discharge their duties without fear. The battle for the freedom of expression has to be fought to the bitter end no matter how many of us fall to the assassins' bullets. In the end it is we, wielders of the pen, who will win and not thugs armed with AK–47 rifles.

April 1991

Ever since the ninth Lok Sabha was dissolved and fresh elections were announced I have been rung up periodically by foreign radio and TV networks to comment on their likely outcome. I hedge my answers with lots of ifs and buts because I am as confused about the future as anyone else. However, when they ask me whether or not I am for having elections in the Punjab and Assam, I can't get away with vague generalities: the answer has to be yes or no. Since I am not well acquainted with conditions in Assam, I answer honestly: "I do not know." About the Punjab hitherto my answer has been "no, there is far too much violence in several districts and little likelihood of people being able to vote freely and without fear." Those who have heard me have accused me of being unfair to my home state by supporting those who persist in denying its right to have a democratic government. The argument for elections runs somewhat as follows: we must break the impasse by opening a dialogue with supporters of Khalistan like Mann and the terrorist groups; that once hot-headed people are given responsibility, they cool down and act responsibly; and that at the worst, if they persist in their secessionist demands, there is nothing to stop the central government from stepping in and dismissing them. This is how I interpret Chandra Shekhar and his government's approach to the Punjab. I regard it as both foolhardy and dishonest. Foolhardy, because on the one hand Chandra Shekhar maintains that he will only open dialogue within the framework of the Constitution; on the other, he negotiates with people who openly proclaim defiance of the Constitution and want to break away from India. It must be abundantly clear to him that as long as thousands of armed young men roam about the countryside, elections cannot be free or fair. If there is no violence, it will only be because no one will dare to question the all-pervading presence of armed gangsters. The police and para-military forces may see that no violence erupts during the poll, but who will protect the people from vengeance after the law-keeping forces are withdrawn? Why I think Chandra Shekhar is also being dishonest is that he knows that the separatists will see that no Congress, Communist or BJP candidates win in any constituency. He will thus bequeath a solid separatist representation from the Punjab to the Lok Sabha to the man who will succeed him as Prime Minister. And worse, if elections are also held to the State Assembly, almost certainly the first thing Mann and his supporters will do is to pass a resolution demanding Khalistan and give a semblance of legitimate demand. Is the gamble worth taking?

December 1991

L ast week I had the privilege of hosting a meeting of some of the top politicians and journalists of the Punjab. They represented different shades of opinion: Akali, Congress, BJP and Communist. They did not wish to be named, but some day, if they allow me, I will divulge their identities. All of them were important enough to be escorted by swarms of security men : Black Cats, CRPF, Delhi Police. My little apartment looked a fortress besieged. They did all the talking; except for an occasional query, I did all the listening. I put down what they said as representative of the feelings of common Punjabis barring rabid elements led by Simranjit Singh Mann and dacoits who go under the names of different gangs of terrorists.

They were of one opinion that in Punjab, Pakistan is fighting a war by proxy against India. There was some difference of opinion about the number of training camps in Pakistan, but irrefutable evidence that they exist, train young Indians in the use of sophisticated weapons, furnish them with arms and ammunition free or at throwaway prices and help them to infiltrate back into India. The weaponry now includes not only automatic rifles but rocket launchers and shells that can incapacitate tanks, and stringer missiles as well. The fifth column that Pakistan is building up in our Punjab could become the most dangerous hazard to us in the event of hostilities breaking out. This was the only point on which I expressed my reservations as I feel that far too often we use Pakistan as an alibi when we can't handle our own affairs. However, they stuck to their opinion and maintained that Pakistan was most certainly involved in Punjab's turmoil.

The second point they made was that in districts

bordering on Pakistan, there is virtually no government and lawlessness prevails. People are robbed and murdered at will, their women folk abducted, raped and maimed; money extorted from shopkeepers, tradesmen, professionals and landowners. The robbers have no dearth of recruits; they offer them double the wages they can get as policemen or *jawans*, more if they have received training in the army or the police, and if killed in encounters, their families are handsomely compensated. Despite this, the common peasantry of the districts of Majha is throughly fed up with the depredations of these gangsters and only needs a strong leader who can bring them together to combat them.

Under the circumstances, to talk of holding elections in the Punjab is highly irresponsible and dangerous. People should not be fooled by Mann's argument that the last Lok Sabha elections had record turnout and there was no violence. They were by no means free or fair because the people were coerced by the presence of armed gangs to go and vote for candidates of Mann's Panthic Party. No amount of police or military presence— which perforce can only be for a few days during the election campaign and polling—will give the necessary reassurance to the people to make their choice freely. There must be no elections in the Punjab till terrorists have been wiped out otherwise the state legislature will be heavily dominated by subversive elements who will inevitably act against national interests.

Akali factions have lost all credibility among the Sikhs. Most of them, including Tohra and Talwandi having suffered bullet wounds at the hands of killers, are now thoroughly demoralised and unwilling to face them. Badal has tried to gain favour with them by attending *bhog* ceremonies of slain killers misnamed *shaheeds* (martyrs). Not one of the top Akali leaders has been bold enough to condemn the killing of innocent men, women and children and only harps against police excesses and organised fake encounters. The only exception is Amarinder Singh of Patiala who has, at long last, spoken and written against the dacoits masquerading as Khalistanis.

The immediate need is to strengthen the hands of the Punjab police, which, being predominantly Sikh, is in a better position to combat killer gangs, also largely Sikh. They have better chances of support from the Sikh peasantry than the CRPF or the Border Security Force which are looked upon as outsiders since most of them cannot even speak Punjabi.

A big mistake is to put captured gun-men and their uncommitted supporters in the same jail. We know from people who are put in close proximity, their leaders use the opportunity to indoctrinate novices into becoming hardliners. This has been amply proved by the Punjab experience: young boys who spent a few months in prison with hardened criminals, come out as hardened criminals. They should therefore be dispersed to jails outside the state.

The Punjab problem has to be tackled on all fronts: emotional, religious, economic and political. It is not as insolvable as it may appear to outsiders. The one redeeming feature of the Punjab scenario is that far from dividing the Hindu from the Sikh, goondaism has brought the two communities closer to each other than ever before. All is not lost: what the Punjab needs today is a strong, enlightened government willing to combine stern methods with compassion.

December 1991

The Home Minister called an all party meeting to advise him how to get the better of terrorism in the Punjab. Those who matter turned down his invitation. Those who accepted mattered less but let off a lot of hot steam. I don't know what the minister got out of the exercise.

The questions were simple: Why does terrorism continue? What can we do to combat it? The answers were not so simple. Terrorists are no longer religiously or politically motivated; they are gangsters who rob, abduct and extort money, commit rape and murder. They cover up their thuggery by giving themselves fancy titles and pretend religious and political motives to gain some legitimacy. What still rankles in Sikh minds is Operation Bluestar and unpunished murders of thousands of innocent people following the assassination of Mrs. Gandhi. Nothing much can be done about them now. However, in order to deprive terrorists of any excuse to continue their depredations, the least the government can do is to express official regret for "Bluestar" and withdraw its spurious White Paper. It could also disassociate itself from men named by several non-official commissions of inquiry for having played nefarious roles in the November 1984 killings. Then it must state clearly and categorically that there will be no dialogue with representatives of gangsters or with supporters of Khalistan. Successive governments have been very inconsistent in their dealings with them. They must realise that by extending them invitations for talks, they sap the morale of the police.

The moot question is why, despite the massive deployment of the army, para-military forces and the police, terrorists continue to get fresh recruits to their

149

ranks? Again the answer is simple. The presence of armed might has failed to protect life and property of the common people and they have no option but to come to terms with terrorists. For this the government can only blame itself. There also have been many incidents of violation of human rights, extortion and torture in prison of suspects. This has turned many law-abiding citizens into terrorists.

Once elections take place, new leaders will emerge. A new accord covering Chandigarh, border adjustments and distribution of river waters must be made with them. Following a new accord, the government must embark on a massive plan of industrialisation with the help of Punjabi NRIs who are more than eager to do something positive for their home state.

January 1992

The agenda document on Jammu and Kashmir and the Punjab issued for the consideration of the National Integration Council makes a grim reading. It admits that the situation in the Valley of the Jhelum poses "the gravest threat to national unity and integrity," that over the last three years thousands of terrorists have received training in Pakistan; and Pakistan is now fighting a proxy war against India with trained terrorists using sophisticated weapons like rockets, Kalashnikovs, grenades and mines and engaging our security forces; that the feeling of alienation in the Valley is higher than ever before; that terrorist violence has paralysed the economy; and Pakistan is carrying on vigorous anti-India propaganda in international forums like the United Nations, NAM and Islamic organisations.

Punjab has been troubled for too long now. In the last ten years over 10,000 innocent people have been murdered: the figures for the year just ended are higher than those of the years before, approximating 3,000 killed. That gives the lie to the claim that with the deployment of the army, the number of killings has sharply declined. It has in fact increased and terrorists have no dearth of fresh recruits to join their gangs. In this state, terrorists have specially aimed their guns at policemen and their families; they are enforcing in their diktats on how people should dress, what they should eat and drink; how banks should conduct their businesses; what orders magistrates and judges should pass.

As in the case of Kashmir so in the case of Punjab, the course of subversive activities is chalked out by a conclave sitting in Pakistan. They are determined to see that no elections take place in the state.

Already 24 candidates for the Vidhan Sabha and three for the Lok Sabha have been slain. Neverthless, we have committed ourselves to holding fresh elections next month.

What constructive suggestions can the National Integration Council, consisting of over 140 members meeting for a few hours, make? What are the options open to us? Only three. One, to go on doing what we are doing to contain terrorism by deployment of larger forces; two, to go to war against Pakistan and hopefully settle the matter once for all times—a course which only lunatics would advise; and finally to open a dialogue with Pakistan on the future of the Valley (excluding Ladakh and Jammu) and arrive at some settlement which would be acceptable to the people of the Valley and be endorsed by both India and Pakistan. Once this is achieved, Pakistan will lose interest in our Punjab and Khalistani militants will lose their base and sustenance.

February 1992

So much has been happening in the Punjab at the same time that it looks like a modern impressionistic painting. No one can be sure what it represents. One thing is sure—it will have elections in a few days. How many people will vote (or be allowed to vote without fear), how many parties will put up candidates openly and how many will do so surreptitiously, no one really knows. The decision ultimately rests with the militants who continue to call the shots. Their main targets will be the Akalis who, despite their bluster and bravado, have proved themselves not only to be muddle-headed but chicken-hearted as well. Will they leave the field wide open to the Congress and the BJP? That will be a great pity. I am sure what the Punjab needs is an Akali government committed to the Constitution led by Amarinder, Barnala, Badal or Sukhjinder. It will be in the best position to contain terrorism.

What about the terrorists? Haven't they had enough of killing and being killed? My information, for whatever it is worth, is that they have and would be happy to make an honourable settlement. Rajesh Pilot, the only minister from the centre to visit the most terrorist-infested areas of Taran Taran, was given a tumultuous welcome. He dispensed with his security and had long talks with their leaders. It transpired that what they asked for was release of their comrades held in custody without trial, cessation of police and army activities against them, implementation of the Rajiv-Longowal accord and setting up of a major industry in every district. No one spoke of Khalistan. None of this seems unreasonable or impracticable. All it needs is courage to go ahead. Let us have no more consultations with Chief Ministers or political parties. No more commissions to go into this or that. Let the government make whatever decisions they deem fair to Punjab, Haryana, Himachal and Rajasthan regarding Chandigarh, boundary adjustments, distribution of river waters and present them to the states concerned as final. Let them appoint one minister who has no other job except to see they are implemented within a few months. At the moment the man most acceptable to the central government as well as the parties concerned is Rajesh Pilot. Let him pilot this package deal to bring it to a happy conclusion. There will be a lot of mischief-makers raising all kinds of frivolous objections: there will be carping and criticism within the cabinet. It should be ignored. Let dogs bark but get the caravan of peace to resume its march.

February 1992

When Punjabis celebrate some great achievement they dance the *bhangra* and yell *O balley! balley!* The last election does not call for any sort of celebration. Less than a quarter of the people went to vote: the bullet and the boycott did in fact score over the ballot and common sense. The gains can be counted on two fingers, the losses on the fingers of both hands. First, the gains. Governor's rule is over; an elected chief minister and his cabinet take over the administration. The Congress party gains another twelve seats in the Lok Sabha and edges closer to the half-mark. A few more wins and it may free itself of reliance on the backward-looking BJP, reckless socialists and regional parties. That is about all there is on the plus side. The debit side has many more items. The most important is the absence of a mandate. Beant Singh and the Congress Party do not in fact reflect the wishes of the people of the Punjab—only of less than 20 per cent of them. The blame does not lie with them but with the Akalis who threw away a golden opportunity to assert their numerical superiority. They succumbed to threats of violence issued by terrorists and will hereafter remain mouthpieces of gun-toting gangsters. They will not even be allowed to retire into pastoral oblivion as many would like to but be bullied by terrorists into launching agitations and keeping the Punjab pot on the boil. The Akalis have good reasons to shift some of the blame on to the central government which did not give them anything to talk about in their election campaign. It will undoubtedly do so now to strengthen the hands of Beant and Company. And inevitably allow Beant to get more mileage out of releasing Akali leaders when he feels more secure in his saddle.

The question that will remain unanswered is will the new set-up be better able to combat terrorism and bring peace to the Punjab? Scarcely so. Without the people's whole hearted co-operation, there is little prospect of nabbing terrorists. The measly turnout at the polls has clearly shown that the peasantry will not stick their necks out for this government and terrorism will continue unabated. There is no occasion to dance the *bhangra*, nothing to yell *balley! balley!* about.

13
Conclusion

Ever since the word Khalistan was coined, I have done my best to enter into dialogue with its supporters to find out exactly what they have in mind. I have failed to meet a single individual who could rationally explain to me its concept, its geographical boundaries, its religious composition and its proposed political and economic set up. I had two long meetings with Ganga Singh Dhillon. His reading of Sikh religion and history was woefully wrong and he evaded answering direct questions. On a visit to England, however, I was able to acquire some documentation on the subject which reveals the total confusion in the minds of its supporters. One is a detailed map of Khalistan—the first that I have seen. It is published in England priced at £2 but no date of publication is mentioned. According to this map, Khalistan will include Jammu, the whole of Himachal Pradesh, Haryana, Delhi, chunks of Uttar Pradesh,

Rajasthan and Saurashtra to give the state an outlet to the sea. By rough reckoning , the Sikh population of this state will be no more than 13 per cent of the total. What kind of Sikh state will this be? Quite clearly, not democratic. Nevertheless, a boxed item explaining the concept describes it as "a sort of paradise on earth". It has ten signatories led by a gentleman named Jaswant Singh Thekedar styling himself as "Defence Minister Khalistan Government". Do Simranjeet Singh Mann and his supporters accept this map as the geographical concept of Khalistan?

My second acquisition is a pamphlet apparently emanating from Pakistan because on its cover it has photographs of the Minister of Religious Affairs of Pakistan visiting Nankana Sahib. Inside is a page entitled "Wait & See". Beneath it in Gurmukhi is an extract alleged to have been taken from *Sau Saakkhee*— a spurious document ascribed to Guru Gobind Singh. From time to time new versions of these so-called prophesies are published to suit aspirants to power. I have two in my possession: one prophesying Maharaja Dalip Singh's return as ruler of the Punjab; another published in 1946 promising the Kingdom to Maharaja Yadavendra Singh. This one prophesies widespread bloodshed, invasion of India by China and Russia and promises the throne of Delhi to the Khalsa. The fabricators of the document did not realise that towns like Ambala did not exist in the time of Guru Gobind Singh: it was a tiny hamlet *Ambwali* raised into a cantonement by the British and renamed Ambala. I will not be surprised if in its next fabrication, Simranjeet Singh Mann's name is inserted as the King of Khalistan.

My third acquisition is a booklet entitled *Raj Kareyga Khalsa*? by Iqbal Kaiser published in Lahore in

1984. It is in Punjabi written in Urdu script. To my chagrin I find it begins with Ajit Caur's article based on what I had seen in Amritsar soon after Operation Bluestar. It gives a brief account of the rise of Bhindranwale, his clash with the Nirankaris and the reasons why the government deliberately created conditions to justify its attack on the Golden Temple. The prospect of Khalistan coming into existence is left with a question mark. What I found amusing was the author's dedication of the copy to Dr. Jagjit Singh in Gurmukhi: instead of giving the venerable propounder of Khalistan's proper surname Chauhan, he writes it as *Choohaan*. A slip perhaps indicating the Doctor's return into the hole of oblivion. How seriously then can anyone take the threat of Khalistan?

What requires serious thought and action however are the ground realities in Punjab. One thing that has not changed is continuing violence; it has been with us since Bhindranwale rose over the Punjab firmament. We had grievously underestimated the number of terrorists and their hold on the peasantry in certain districts. We have been fed with wishful data of the numbers killed or apprehended by handouts issued by the police. The terrorists have managed to murder on an average of between five to a dozen innocent men, women and children daily and rob banks of large sums of money including one haul of Rs. 6 crores. Whatever be the number of terrorists successive police commissioners may claim to have bagged, there seems no noticeable decline in their nefarious activities. What is more disheartening is that so far there is no concrete evidence of a people's movement against terrorism. On the contrary, from the way most terrorists manage to get away after committing crimes, it can be presumed that there is tacit acquiescence, fear or indifference towards them. No one is willing to stick his neck out to pursue them and help the police. When it comes to choosing between terrorists and the police, most people say that they fear the police more than the terrorists.

This is a very unhappy state of affairs because there is little prospect of getting the better of terrorism without the active cooperation of the people. And there can be no lasting solution to Punjab's problems till terrorism is stamped out. Inevitably, combating terrorism must be given top priority.

Fortunately, some steps have been taken in that direction. Tension with Pakistan some time back gave the central government the excuse to mass troops in the districts most affected by terrorism, which were the chief inlets of arms smuggled from Pakistan. One hopes that the Pakistan border has been effectively sealed. The composition of terrorist gangs has also undergone a radical change. Religious fanatics who predominated during the days of Bhindranwale and the period immediately following Operation Bluestar have been largely eliminated. What remain are protagonists of Khalistan, Naxalties, smugglers, robbers and common criminals. The common people may not help the police in pursuing them but they are getting more and more reluctant to provide them means of escape. It should also be noted that targets seem to have changed. Evidently, they have abandoned their earlier plan to terrorise Punjabi Hindus and force them to leave Punjab and in return provoke a Hindu backlash in other parts of India and force Sikhs living there to migrate to Punjab. Their attempt to create a *de facto* Khalistan has failed because the mass of Sikhs has refused to respond to the notion of a separate Sikh state.

Of course, still more needs to be done to wipe out terrorism. The most important of them is to see that Sikh gurdwaras retain their sanctity and are not allowed to become sanctuaries for fugitives from justice or provide platforms for politicians. It is well-known that he who controls the Harimandir (Golden Temple) controls the minds of the Sikhs. Unfortunately, the Harimandir and the adjoining Akal Takht are currently under the control of the SGPC and head priests nominated by it who support the notion of a separate Sikh state and are reluctant to denounce terrorists. This is equally true of several other important Sikh shrines. The cleansing of the gurdwaras is entirely the duty of the Sikh *sangat* (congregation). In most places *sangats* rue the absence of religious fervour that used to pervade their temples before they were politicised. There is reason to hope that these *sangats* will assert themselves and oust priest-politicians as their forefathers ousted heriditary *mahants* from control of their *gurdwaras*. Otherwise they will have to put up with the police regularly entering their temples to apprehend law breakers. There can be no compromise with the principle that where there is a criminal, the police has the right to be.

Two other aspects of the terrorist problem must be borne in mind. First is the influx of young men into their ranks. There is reason to believe that a sizeable number joined them after the killing of innocents in encounters faked by the police. Mr Rebeiro admitted that there have been cases of unidentified people being shot and brutality by the police. This must be put an end to immediately: it is better that 10 murderers escape than kill one innocent person. It is equally important to bring to book people responsible for the killings of Sikhs following the assassination of Mrs Gandhi. So far not one person has been brought to trial for the most horrendous massacre since Independence. On the other hand, some people named as guilty by independent commissions of inquiry have been rewarded with ministerial positions and a clumsy attempt made through the Misra Commission to sweep this murky episode under the carpet of oblivion. It is too much to expect the Sikh community to forgive and forget the murder, mayhem, rape and arson perpetrated on over 5,000 of their co-religionists. It also puts a black spot on the face of the nation. What is worse, it gives justification to the terrorists who can then rightly taunt others to ask: "What justice can Sikhs expect from a government which refuses to punish murderers of Sikhs?" We should realise that crimes unpunished breed criminals.

The second priority after putting down terrorism is to restore Hindu-Sikh relations to what they were before Bhindranwale started making his hateful utterances against the Hindus and his gangsters started desecrating Hindu temples and slaying innocent people. Fortunately, despite the continuing violence over the past five years the vast majority of both communities continue to live in harmony. It is significant that in all this period there has not been a single instance of Sikh mobs attacking Hindus. Unlike what happened after Mrs Gandhi's assassination when Hindu mobs attacked Sikhs; in the Punjab all killings have been carried out by small gangs against individuals. Hindu-Sikh marriages between castes that used to intermarry continue as before. Although the number of Hindu worshippers at Sikh gurdwaras has declined (as has the numbers of Sikhs themselves) they are still to be seen in large numbers.

Sikh pilgrims can still be seen at Hindu places of pilgrimage and taking ritual baths in the Ganga.

It will not take much to further the process of restoring communal harmony. Hindus believing in Sikhism (there are millions of them) should resume worship in Sikh gurdwaras. Even orthodox Hindus should make it a point to visit gurdwaras and thus give Sikhs a feeling of reassurance that they regard Sikhs as a part of their community.

A ccording to *The Statesman* of 22nd May, 1989, criminals who murdered Dr. Ravinder Ravi, writer and professor, in Patiala had four other names on their hit list: Playwright Gurcharan Singh Arshi, Editor of *Nawan Zamana*, CPI leader Jagjit Singh Anand, novelist Kulbir Kang, and myself. Although I have put my name last, I am apparently on the top of this mini hit list. According to leaders of the All India Sikh Students Federation, the Khalistan Commando Force and Khalistan Liberation Force, our heads are to roll because of our "anti-Sikh writings."

I think it is time these killers were told in plain language what is and what is not anti-Sikh. At the risk of being accused of indulging in self-praise, I will start with myself. What the English-speaking world knows of the Sikhs, their religion, history and their achievements is largely through my books published in America and England. All the entries on Sikhism in the *Encyclopaedia Britannica* are mine. I, more than any other person, am called upon by foreign radio and television networks for comments on events in the Punjab, particularly regarding the Sikhs. I have never made myself out to be a man of religion but zealously retain my Sikh identity and am emotionally involved in the Sikhs fortunes. I condemned Bhindranwale because I regarded him as anti-Sikh; I condemned Operation Bluestar because I regarded it as anti-Sikh and anti-nation. I condemn terrorism because killing innocent people is condemned by our gurus as a sin. I make no distinction between Hindu and Sikh victims of violence: my heart goes out to the widows and children who have been deprived of their bread-earners and I do the little I can for them. I know our gurus would approve of that. I oppose Khalistan because I know it will spell disaster for the Sikh community as well as the country. There is nothing anti-Sikh about any of this.

The three other writers on the assassins' hit list are doing more than me in spreading the message of goodwill between the two sister communities. They do so at enormous risks to their lives because they too feel that this is what the gurus would have liked them to do and because they feel it is the best thing to do for the community and country.

And now let me tell our would-be assassins what is anti-Sikh. Killing an old *Jathedar* of the Akal Takht was anti-Sikh. Killing Sant Longowal was anti-Sikh. Killing Master Tara Singh's daughter, Bibi Rajinder Kaur was anti-Sikh. Hanging innocent Hindus was anti-Sikh. I could extend the list of their anti-Sikh activities to several pages. Those who committed these crimes disgraced their gurus and the religion they profess.

Inspite of the massive security that surrounds me wherever I go, they came very close to getting me. The story unfolded itself when I happened to be holidaying in Goa two years ago. Armed police were posted in front and at the rear of my hotel room. Four men accompanied me when I went for a stroll on the beach. I protested to the D.I.G. Police of Goa against this unwarranted intrusion into my privacy. Very gently he explained why I needed so much guarding. The police officer happened to be the one who had interrogated Jinda who had murdered General Vaidya in Pune and then absconded. A year later, he was captured in Delhi. On his person they found a plan of my apartment showing the chair by the window where I normally sit to read and write. Jinda confessed that he had visited my apartment, gone to the kitchen to ask for a glass of water and taken a good look around to mark escape routes. He also admitted that he had followed me up to Kasauli but at village Garkhal, two miles short of Kasauli, felt he was being shadowed and returned to Delhi where he was captured. He is now under sentence of death for the murder of General A. S. Vaidya. He was asked why he wanted to kill me. He admitted that he knew very little about me and had not read anything I had written. But his bosses, who directed him, felt that I had to be eliminated because I was an enemy of Khalistan. Jinda was told that I would be an easy target and would evoke a lot of publicity.

I am not a brave man but being slain by a terrorist does not disturb my night's sleep. Manini Chatterjee of *The Telegraph* and *Sunday* came to get answers to a questionnaire drafted by her editor. The last question was, "How would you like to die?" I answered quite candidly and without bravado, 'I would like to be shot by a Khalistani terrorist. At my age (77), a quick end would be preferable to wasting away with some old-age disease in a hospital. It would also give me the halo of martyrdom and the feeling that I had given my life to preserve the integrity of my motherland. Terrorist threats do not deter

me, and many others like me, from writing what we are
writing and doing what we are doing. If they succeed in
getting us, I am sure many others will rise to continue
this *Dharma Yudh* against these evil men.